# Recipes:
# The Cooking of Spain and Portugal

## Contents

### Foods of the World

TIME-LIFE BOOKS, NEW YORK

# Soups

## Sopa de Ajo
SPICY GARLIC SOUP

To serve 6 to 8

½ cup olive oil
2 tablespoons finely chopped garlic
3 cups coarsely crumbled French or
   Italian bread, trimmed of all crusts
1 teaspoon paprika

6 cups water
¼ teaspoon cayenne pepper
1 teaspoon salt
2 eggs, lightly beaten
1 tablespoon finely chopped parsley
   (optional)

In a heavy 3- to 4-quart saucepan, warm the olive oil over low heat. Add the garlic. Stirring frequently, cook for 2 or 3 minutes, or until the garlic is soft but not brown. Stir in the crumbled bread, raise the heat to moderate and cook until the bread is golden. Be careful not to let it burn. Stir in the paprika, then add the water, cayenne pepper and salt and bring to a boil. Reduce the heat to low and simmer uncovered for 30 minutes.

With a large wooden spoon beat the soup until the bread is thoroughly pulverized. Then slowly pour in the beaten eggs, stirring constantly. Simmer a moment or two (do not let the soup come anywhere near a boil or it will curdle) and taste. The soup should be highly seasoned; add more salt and cayenne pepper if it seems to be too bland. Pour the soup into a heated tureen or individual soup plates and serve it at once, garnished if you like with finely chopped parsley.

## Sopa à Alentejana
CORIANDER AND GARLIC SOUP WITH POACHED EGGS

To serve 4

| | |
|---|---|
| 2 teaspoons finely chopped garlic | 4 to 6 tablespoons lard |
| 1 teaspoon salt, preferably coarse salt | 2 slices homemade-type white bread, trimmed of crusts and each cut |
| ¼ cup finely chopped fresh coriander (*cilantro*) | diagonally into 4 triangles |
| ½ cup olive oil | 4 very fresh eggs |
| | 2 cups boiling water |

Mash the garlic and salt to a paste with a mortar and pestle, or with the back of a wooden spoon. Mash in the coriander and then beat in the olive oil, 1 tablespoon at a time, continuing to beat until the oil is thoroughly absorbed. Divide the mixture among 4 individual soup bowls, and set them aside.

In a heavy 8- to 10-inch skillet, melt 4 tablespoons of the lard over moderate heat until it splutters. Add the bread triangles, and brown them well on both sides adding up to 2 more tablespoons of lard if necessary. Drain on a double thickness of paper towels.

Bring 2 inches of water to a simmer in a 10- to 12-inch skillet. Break 1 egg into a saucer. Holding the dish as close as possible to the water, slide the egg into the skillet. Gently lift the white over the yolk with a large spoon. Following the same procedure and keeping the water at a slow simmer, break the 3 remaining eggs into the saucer one at a time and slide them into the water. Poach the eggs for 3 to 5 minutes, depending on how firm you prefer them; the cooked yolks should remain somewhat soft.

Pour ½ cup of boiling water into each of the soup bowls, add a poached egg and arrange two fried bread triangles beside it. Serve immediately.

NOTE: If your eggs are not farm fresh, cook them in an egg poacher rather than a skillet. Though scarcely traditional, the poacher will produce more predictable results and prevent the possible separation of the egg whites from the yolks.

## Sopa al Cuarto de Hora

"QUARTER-HOUR" CLAM, SHRIMP, HAM AND RICE SOUP

To serve 4 to 6

1 quart water

8 small hard-shelled clams, washed and thoroughly scrubbed

2 tablespoons olive oil

½ cup finely chopped onions

1 teaspoon finely chopped garlic

1 small bay leaf

1 large tomato peeled, seeded and finely chopped (*see huevos a la flamenca, page 68*)

¼ cup finely chopped *serrano* ham, or substitute 1 ounce prosciutto or other lean smoked ham

2 tablespoons finely chopped parsley

¼ cup raw medium or long-grain regular-milled rice or imported short-grain rice

¼ cup dry white wine

⅛ teaspoon ground saffron or saffron threads crushed with a mortar and pestle or with the back of a spoon

½ teaspoon fresh lemon juice

8 medium-sized raw shelled shrimp, cut into ½-inch pieces

1 hard-cooked egg, finely chopped

In a heavy 3- to 4-quart saucepan, bring 1 quart of water to a boil. Drop in the clams, cover tightly and boil briskly for 5 to 10 minutes, or until the shells open. With a slotted spoon, transfer the clams to a plate, remove the clams and discard the shells. (Discard any clams that remain closed.) Set the clams aside and reserve the cooking liquid.

Meanwhile, prepare the *sofrito:* In a heavy 8- to 10-inch skillet, heat the oil over moderate heat until a light haze forms above it. Add the onions, garlic and bay leaf. Stirring occasionally, cook for 5 minutes, or until the onions are soft and transparent but not brown. Add the tomatoes, ham and parsley, raise the heat and cook briskly for about 5 minutes, or until most of the liquid in the pan evaporates and the mixture is thick enough to hold its shape lightly in a spoon. Set aside off the heat.

Strain the clam cooking liquid through a fine sieve, and return it to the saucepan. Add the *sofrito*, rice, wine, saffron and lemon juice, bring to a boil over high heat, and reduce the heat to low. Stir once or twice, partially cover the pan and simmer for about 15 minutes or until the rice is tender. (This cooking period is the quarter hour from which the soup gets its name.) Add the shrimp, egg and clams and simmer for 2 or 3 minutes longer until the shrimp turn pink. Taste and season with salt and pepper if desired. Serve at once from a heated tureen or individual soup plates.

# Gazpacho

COLD FRESH VEGETABLE SOUP

To serve 6 to 8

SOUP

2 medium-sized cucumbers, peeled and coarsely chopped

5 medium-sized tomatoes, peeled and coarsely chopped

1 large onion, coarsely chopped

1 medium-sized green pepper, deribbed, seeded and coarsely chopped

2 teaspoons finely chopped garlic

4 cups coarsely crumbled French or Italian bread, trimmed of crusts

4 cups cold water

¼ cup red wine vinegar

4 teaspoons salt

4 tablespoons olive oil

1 tablespoon tomato paste

In a deep bowl, combine the coarsely chopped cucumbers, tomatoes, onion and green pepper, garlic and crumbled bread, and mix together thoroughly. Then stir in the water, vinegar and salt. Ladle the mixture, about 2 cups at a time, into the jar of a blender and blend at high speed for 1 minute, or until reduced to a smooth purée. Pour the purée into a bowl and with a whisk beat in the olive oil and tomato paste.

(To make the soup by hand, purée the vegetable and bread mixture in a food mill or, with the back of a large spoon, rub it through a sieve set over a bowl. Discard any pulp left in the mill or sieve. Beat the olive oil and tomato paste into the purée.)

Cover the bowl tightly with foil or plastic wrap and refrigerate for at least 2 hours, or until thoroughly chilled. Just before serving, whisk or stir the soup lightly to recombine it. Then ladle it into a large chilled tureen or individual soup plates.

GARNISH

1 cup ¼-inch bread cubes, trimmed of crusts

½ cup finely chopped onions

½ cup peeled and finely chopped cucumbers

½ cup finely chopped green peppers

Accompany the *gazpacho* with the bread cubes and the vegetable garnishes presented in separate serving bowls to be added to the soup at the discretion of each diner.

NOTE: If you prefer crisp croutons for the garnish, fry the bread cubes. In a 6- to 8-inch skillet, heat ¼ cup of olive oil over moderate heat until a light haze forms above it. Drop in the bread cubes and, turning them frequently, cook them until they are crisp and golden brown on all sides. Drain on paper towels and cool.

## Potaje de Vigilia
CHICK-PEA, COD AND SPINACH SOUP

To serve 6 to 8

2 cups (1 pound) dried chick-peas
(garbanzos)
½ pound salt cod
3 quarts water
1 cup finely chopped onions
1 large bay leaf
1 teaspoon salt
1½ pounds fresh spinach, washed,
trimmed and coarsely chopped, or
substitute two 10-ounce packages
frozen leaf spinach, thoroughly
defrosted, drained, squeezed dry,
and coarsely chopped
4 whole blanched almonds, toasted
(see bôlo de amêndoa à algarvia,
page 98), and coarsely chopped
1 teaspoon finely chopped garlic
2 hard-cooked egg yolks
¼ cup olive oil
1 slice white bread, preferably
homemade-type, trimmed of crusts
and cut into ½ inch squares
2 tablespoons flour
1 tablespoon paprika

Starting a day ahead, wash the chick-peas in a sieve under cold running water, then place them in a bowl or pan and add enough cold water to cover them by 1 inch. Soak at room temperature for at least 12 hours.

At the same time, place the cod in a glass, enameled or stainless-steel bowl or pan. Cover it with cold water and soak for at least 12 hours, changing the water 3 or 4 times.

Drain the chick-peas in a sieve or colander. Pour 3 quarts of water into a heavy 5- to 6-quart casserole and add the chick-peas, ½ cup of the onions, the bay leaf and salt. The water should cover the chick-peas by about 2 inches. Add more, if necessary. Bring to a boil over high heat, reduce the heat to low, and simmer partially covered for 1½ hours.

Meanwhile, drain the cod and rinse under cold running water. Place it in a saucepan, add enough fresh water to cover the fish by 1 inch, and bring to a boil over high heat. (Taste the water. If it seems excessively salty, drain, cover with fresh water, and bring to a boil again.) Reduce the heat to low, and simmer uncovered for about 20 minutes, or until the fish flakes easily when prodded gently with a fork. Drain thoroughly. With a small knife, remove and discard the skin and any bones, then separate the fish into coarse flakes. Set the cod aside.

Drop the fresh spinach into 2 quarts of boiling water, and boil briskly for 5 minutes. Drain in a large sieve or colander, and when the spinach is cool enough to handle squeeze vigorously to rid it of all moisture. (Frozen spinach should not be boiled but simply defrosted, squeezed dry, and chopped.)

With a large mortar and pestle or with the back of a large spoon, mash the almonds and garlic to a paste. Add the egg yolks and continue to mash until the mixture is smooth.

In a heavy 10- to 12-inch skillet, heat the olive oil over moderate heat until a light haze forms above it. Add the bread and, turning the pieces frequently, brown them lightly on all sides. With a slotted spoon, transfer these croutons to paper towels to drain. Add the remaining ½ cup of onions to the fat remaining in the pan and, stirring frequently, cook for 5 minutes, or until they are soft and transparent but not brown. Sprinkle the flour over the onions, and cook for a minute or two until it browns lightly. Add the spinach and cook, stirring, for 2 minutes.

Crumble the croutons, and mash them into the almond and garlic paste. Then stir the crouton mixture into the spinach. Add the paprika and cook, stirring briskly, for 2 or 3 minutes.

When the peas have cooked their allotted 1½ hours, stir the cod and the spinach mixture into the simmering soup and cook, partially covered, for 20 minutes longer. Then remove the bay leaf, taste for seasoning and serve in a heated tureen or individual soup plates.

NOTE: This soup is traditionally served on Good Friday and other fast days, hence the name "soup of the vigil."

## Canja
CHICKEN SOUP WITH LEMON AND MINT

To serve 6

| | |
|---|---|
| A 3½- to 4-pound stewing fowl, securely trussed | 1½ teaspoons salt |
| The fowl's giblets—heart, gizzard and liver—finely chopped | 3 tablespoons raw medium or long grain regular-milled rice, or imported short grain rice |
| 2 quarts water | ¼ cup fresh lemon juice |
| 1 cup finely chopped onions | 6 tablespoons finely cut fresh mint |

Place the chicken and its giblets in a heavy 3- to 4-quart casserole. Pour in the water and bring to a boil over high heat, meanwhile skimming off the foam and scum as they rise to the surface. Add the onions and salt and reduce the heat to low. Simmer partially covered for 2½ hours, then add the rice and simmer for 30 minutes or until the chicken and rice are tender.

Remove the casserole from the heat and transfer the chicken to a plate. When the bird is cool enough to handle, remove the skin with a small knife or your fingers. Cut or pull the meat away from the bones. Discard the skin and bones, and cut the meat into strips about ⅛ inch wide and 1 inch long.

Just before serving, return the chicken to the casserole, add the lemon juice and taste for seasoning. Bring to a simmer and cook only long enough to heat the chicken through. Place a tablespoon of the cut mint in each of six individual serving bowls, ladle the soup over it and serve at once.

## Sopa da Panela

GARLIC SOUP WITH CHICK-PEAS, MINT AND CROUTONS

To serve 4

1 cup dried chick-peas (garbanzos), or substitute 1½ cups canned chick-peas
½ cup olive oil
2 slices homemade-type white bread, trimmed of crusts and cut into ½-inch squares
2 teaspoons finely chopped garlic

½ teaspoon salt, preferably coarse salt
⅓ cup finely chopped fresh mint leaves
¼ cup finely chopped fresh parsley
1 quart *cozido* stock *(page 55)*, or substitute 1 quart chicken stock, fresh or canned
4 mint sprigs

Starting a day ahead, wash the dried chick-peas in a sieve under cold running water, place them in a large bowl or pan, and add enough cold water to cover them by 2 inches. Soak at room temperature for at least 8 hours. Drain the peas and place them in a heavy 2- to 3-quart saucepan. Add enough fresh water to cover them completely and bring to a boil over high heat. Reduce the heat to low and simmer partially covered for 2 to 2½ hours, or until the peas are tender but still intact. Replenish the liquid with boiling water from time to time if necessary. (Canned chick-peas need only be drained and rinsed under cold running water.)

Meanwhile, in a heavy 8- to 10-inch skillet, heat ¼ cup of the olive oil over high heat until a light haze forms above it. Add the bread squares, lower the heat to moderate and cook, turning them frequently, until they are golden brown on all sides. With a slotted spoon, transfer the croutons to a double thickness of paper towels to drain.

With a mortar and pestle or the back of a large spoon, mash the garlic and salt to a paste in the bottom of a heavy mixing bowl. Beat in the mint, parsley, and then the remaining ¼ cup of olive oil, 1 tablespoon at a time. Continue to beat until the oil is thoroughly absorbed. Bring the stock to a boil in a large saucepan. Add the chick-peas, reduce the heat and simmer for 3 or 4 minutes to heat them through.

To serve, transfer the garlic mixture to a heated tureen. Pour the soup into the tureen, stir with a large spoon to distribute the garlic mixture evenly, and scatter the croutons on top. Garnish with mint.

## Sopa Juliana
VEGETABLE SOUP WITH GARLIC

To serve 6 to 8

SOUP
1/4 pound white cabbage, cored and finely shredded
2 large carrots, scraped and cut into julienne strips 1 1/2 inches long and 1/8 inch wide
1 medium-sized white turnip, peeled and cut into julienne strips 1 1/2 inches long and 1/8 inch wide
1 medium-sized onion, peeled and cut into 1/8-inch-thick slices
1 small bay leaf
1 tablespoon salt
2 quarts water

In a heavy 4- to 5-quart casserole, combine the cabbage, carrots, turnip, sliced onion, bay leaf, salt and water. Bring to a boil over high heat, reduce the heat to low, and simmer partially covered for 30 minutes.

SOFRITO
6 tablespoons olive oil
1 cup finely chopped onions
1 teaspoon finely chopped garlic
2 medium-sized tomatoes, peeled, seeded and finely chopped (see *huevos a la flamenca, page 68*), or substitute 2/3 cup chopped, drained, canned Italian tomatoes
1 tablespoon finely chopped parsley
1 medium-sized potato, peeled and cut into julienne strips 1 1/2 inches long and 1/8 inch wide
1/2 cup fresh green peas (1/2 pound) or 1/2 cup frozen peas, thoroughly defrosted

Meanwhile, make the *sofrito*. Heat the olive oil over moderate heat in a heavy 8-to 10-inch skillet. When a light haze forms above it, add the chopped onions and garlic to the oil and, stirring frequently, cook for 5 minutes, or until the onions are soft and transparent but not brown. Stir in the tomatoes and the parsley, bring to a boil and cook briskly, uncovered, until almost all of the liquid in the pan has evaporated.

Stir the *sofrito* into the simmering soup, add the julienned potato and continue cooking for 20 minutes, then add the peas and cook for 5 to 10 minutes more, or until the vegetables are tender. Taste for seasoning and serve at once from a heated tureen or in individual soup plates.

# Fabada Asturiana
BEAN SOUP WITH SAUSAGES

To serve 6

4 to 5 quarts water

2 cups (1 pound) dried fava beans or dried white kidney beans

2 cups coarsely chopped onions

1 tablespoon finely chopped garlic

¼ pound lean salt pork, in one piece with rind removed

½ pound *serrano* ham, or substitute prosciutto or other lean smoked ham, in one piece

3 *chorizos,* or substitute ½ pound other garlic-seasoned smoked pork sausage

3 *morcillas,* or substitute ½ pound other blood sausage

⅛ teaspoon ground saffron or saffron threads crushed with a mortar and pestle or with the back of a spoon

Salt

Freshly ground black pepper

In a heavy 8- to 10-quart casserole, bring 2 quarts of the water to a boil over high heat. Drop in the beans and boil them briskly uncovered for 2 minutes. Then remove the casserole from the heat and let the beans soak for 1 hour. Drain the beans in a sieve or colander set over a large bowl and return them to the casserole. Measure the bean-soaking liquid, add to it enough additional water to make 4 quarts and pour it into the casserole. Add the onions, garlic, and salt pork and bring to a boil over high heat, meanwhile skimming off the foam as it rises to the surface. Reduce the heat to low and simmer partially covered for 1 hour. Add the ham and simmer about 1 hour longer, or until the beans are barely tender.

Meanwhile, place the *chorizos* in an 8- to 10-inch skillet and prick them in two or three places with the point of a small, sharp knife. Add enough cold water to cover them completely and bring to a boil over high heat. Then reduce the heat to low and simmer uncovered for 5 minutes. Drain the sausages on paper towels.

When the soup has cooked for its allotted 2 hours, drop in the *chorizos* and *morcillas,* stir in the saffron, and cook 30 minutes longer. Taste and season liberally with salt and a few grindings of pepper. Then with a slotted spoon, transfer the salt pork, ham and sausages to a plate. Cut the pork and ham into ½-inch cubes and slice the sausages into ½-inch-thick rounds. Return the meat to the soup and simmer for 2 or 3 minutes. Traditionally, *fabada* is accompanied by a cornbread similar to the Portuguese *broa (Recipe Index)* and glasses of sparkling apple cider.

# Caldo Gallego

WHITE BEAN, TURNIP GREEN AND POTATO SOUP

To serve 6

1 cup dried white beans, preferably white kidney or Great Northern
2 to 3 quarts water
1/2 pound *serrano* ham, cut into 1/2-inch cubes, or substitute prosciutto or other lean smoked ham or pork butt
2 ounces salt pork in one piece, with rind removed
1/2 cup finely chopped onions
2 teaspoons salt
2 *chorizos*, or substitute 1/3 pound other garlic-seasoned smoked pork sausage
1/2 pound turnip greens, washed, trimmed and coarsely shredded
2 small potatoes, peeled and cut into 1/4-inch dice

In a heavy 3- to 4-quart casserole, bring 2 quarts of water to a boil over high heat. Drop in the beans and boil them briskly for 2 minutes. Then remove the pot from the heat and let the beans soak for 1 hour.

Drain the beans in a sieve or colander set over a bowl and return them to the casserole. Measure the soaking liquid and add enough fresh water to make 2 quarts. Pour the water into the casserole, add the ham, salt pork, onions and salt, and bring to a boil over high heat. Reduce the heat to low and simmer partially covered for 1 1/2 hours.

When the beans have cooked their allotted 1 1/2 hours, add the sausages, turnip greens and potatoes and continue to cook, partially covered for 30 minutes longer, or until the beans and potatoes are tender. With a slotted spoon, remove the sausages and salt pork. Slice the sausages into 1/4-inch-thick rounds and return them to the soup. Discard the pork. Taste for seasoning and serve at once from a heated tureen or individual soup plates.

NOTE: This is one version of a classic Galician dish. In other versions, smoked pork shoulder and salt pork are boiled together; sausage is added during the last part of the cooking. The meats are then removed and set aside, and chopped turnip greens, white beans, and diced potatoes are simmered in the remaining broth. The soup that results is served as *caldo gallego*.

The reserved smoked pork and sausages are sliced and served with cooked whole turnip greens and boiled potatoes as a main course known as *lacón con grelos*. The Galician version of the *cocido*, called *pote gallego*, is made with all the above ingredients plus veal and chicken.

## Caldo Verde

POTATO AND KALE SOUP WITH SAUSAGE

To serve 4 to 6

½ pound fresh kale or collard greens
4 ounces *linguiça* or substitute 4 ounces of *chorizo* or any other garlic-seasoned smoked pork sausage
3 medium-sized potatoes (about 1 pound), peeled and sliced into ¼-inch-thick rounds
6 cups water
2 teaspoons salt
½ cup olive oil
¼ teaspoon freshly ground black pepper

Wash the greens under cold running water. With a sharp knife trim away any bruised or blemished spots and strip the leaves from their stems. Bunch the leaves together and shred them into the finest possible strips. Set aside.

Place the sausages in a small skillet and prick them in two or three places with the point of a knife. Add enough water to cover them and bring to a boil over high heat. Reduce the heat to low and simmer for 15 minutes. Drain the sausages on paper towels, slice into ¼-inch rounds, and set aside.

Combine the potatoes, water and salt in a 4- to 5-quart saucepan and bring to a boil over high heat. Reduce the heat to moderate and cook uncovered for 15 minutes, or until the potatoes when tested can be easily mashed against the sides of the pan. With a slotted spoon, transfer the potatoes to a bowl and mash them to a smooth purée with a fork. Return the potatoes to the liquid in the pan, stir in the olive oil and pepper and bring to a boil over high heat. Add the greens and boil uncovered for 3 or 4 minutes. Then drop in the reserved sausages and simmer for a minute or two to heat them through. Serve at once, accompanied by a plate of *broa (Recipe Index)*.

# Seafood

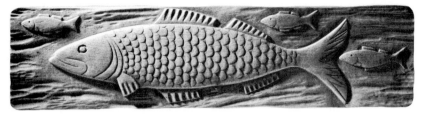

## Bacalao al Ajo Arriero

SALT COD WITH TOMATOES, ONIONS AND GARLIC

To serve 6

2 pounds salt cod
1 cup olive oil
2½ cups finely chopped onions
9 medium-sized tomatoes, peeled,
  seeded and finely chopped (see
*huevos a la flamenca, page 68*), or
  substitute 3 cups chopped,
  drained, canned tomatoes
4 teaspoons finely chopped garlic
¼ teaspoon freshly ground black
  pepper

Starting a day ahead, shred the cod as finely as possible by tearing it into strips and pieces with your fingers. Then place it in a glass, enameled or stainless-steel bowl and cover it with cold water. Soak for at least 12 hours, changing the water 3 or 4 times and each time squeezing the cod vigorously and pulling it into finer and finer shreds. Drain thoroughly.

In a heavy 10- to 12-inch skillet heat ½ cup of the olive oil over high heat until a light haze forms above it. Stir in the cod and ½ cup of the onions and cook, stirring constantly, until the oil becomes milky white. Immediately reduce the heat to moderate and cook uncovered for 30 minutes, or until most of the liquid in the pan has evaporated. (The cod and onions should not be allowed to brown.)

Meanwhile, in another heavy 10- to 12-inch skillet, heat the remaining ½ cup of oil over moderate heat until a light haze forms above it. Add the remaining 2 cups of onions and, stirring frequently, cook for 8 to 10 minutes, or until they are soft and light brown. Stir in the tomatoes, raise the heat and bring to a boil. Stirring and mashing the vegetables with a large spoon, cook briskly until most of the liquid in the pan evaporates and the mixture is thick enough to hold its shape lightly in the spoon.

Stir the tomato mixture, garlic and pepper into the cod, cover the skillet tightly and simmer over low heat for 5 minutes. Let the cod rest, covered, off the heat for at least 15 minutes. Although *bacalao al ajo arriero* may be served hot, in Spain it is often served at room temperature.

## Bolinhos de Bacalhau

CODFISH CAKES WITH PARSLEY, CORIANDER AND MINT

To serve 3 to 6

1 pound salt cod

2 cups coarsely crumbled day-old
French or Italian bread, trimmed
of all crusts

3/4 cup olive oil

1/4 cup finely chopped fresh coriander
(*cilantro*)

1 tablespoon finely chopped parsley

1/2 teaspoon finely chopped fresh mint

2 tablespoons paprika

1 teaspoon salt

1/8 teaspoon freshly ground black
pepper

2 garlic cloves, peeled and cut
lengthwise into halves

6 parsley sprigs

6 freshly poached eggs (optional)

Starting a day ahead, place the cod in a glass, enamel or stainless-steel pan or bowl. Cover it with cold water and soak for at least 12 hours, changing the water 3 or 4 times.

Drain the cod, rinse under cold running water, place it in a saucepan and add enough fresh water to cover the fish by 1 inch. Bring to a boil over high heat. (Taste the water. If it seems excessively salty, drain, cover with fresh water, and bring to a boil again.) Reduce the heat to low and simmer uncovered for about 20 minutes, or until the fish flakes easily when prodded gently with a fork.

Meanwhile, in a large bowl, combine the bread and 1/2 cup of the olive oil. Beat and mash them together until the bread has absorbed all the oil, then set aside.

Drain the cod thoroughly. When it is cool enough to handle, remove and discard any skin and bones. Then shred the fish finely with your fingers or a table fork and place it in a mixing bowl. Add the coriander, chopped parsley, mint, paprika, salt, pepper and reserved bread, and beat vigorously with a large spoon until the ingredients are thoroughly combined. With lightly moistened hands shape the mixture into 6 flat round cakes, about 3½ inches in diameter and 1/2 inch thick.

In a heavy 12-inch skillet, heat the remaining 1/4 cup of olive oil over moderate heat until a light haze forms above it. Add the garlic and, stirring frequently, cook for 2 or 3 minutes, or until golden brown. Then remove and discard them. Add the codfish cakes to the garlic-flavored oil and cook over moderate heat for about 3 minutes on each side turning them carefully with a metal spatula. When they are a golden brown on both sides, transfer them to a heated platter, garnish with parsley sprigs, and serve at once. Traditionally, each cake is topped with a freshly poached egg before serving.

# Bacalhau à Gomes de Sá

SALT COD WITH POTATOES, ONIONS AND BLACK OLIVES

To serve 4 to 6

1½ pounds salt cod
1 tablespoon plus 1 cup olive oil
6 medium-sized potatoes, peeled
4 medium-sized onions, cut
    crosswise into ⅛-inch slices

and separated into rings
½ teaspoon finely chopped garlic
18 to 20 pitted black olives
5 hard-cooked eggs, cut crosswise
    into ¼-inch slices
2 tablespoons finely chopped parsley

Starting a day ahead, place the cod in a glass, enamel or stainless-steel bowl. Cover it with cold water and soak for at least 12 hours, changing the water three or four times.

Preheat the oven to 200°. With a pastry brush, coat the bottom and sides of a casserole 8 inches in diameter and 4 inches deep with 1 tablespoon of olive oil. Drop the potatoes into a pot with enough lightly salted boiling water to cover them completely. Boil briskly until they are tender but not falling apart. Drain, peel and cut the potatoes into ¼-inch slices. Set aside.

Drain the cod, rinse under cold running water, place it in a saucepan and add enough fresh water to cover the fish by 1 inch. Bring to a boil over high heat. (Taste the water. If it seems excessively salty, drain, cover with fresh water, and bring to a boil again.) Reduce the heat to low and simmer uncovered for about 20 minutes, or until the fish flakes easily when prodded gently with a fork. Drain thoroughly. With a small knife, remove and discard any skin and bones and separate the fish into coarse flakes. Set aside.

In a heavy 10- to 12-inch skillet, heat ½ cup of the oil over moderate heat until a light haze forms above it. Add the onion rings. Stirring frequently, cook for 5 minutes, or until they are soft and transparent but not brown. Stir in the garlic and remove the skillet from the heat.

To assemble, spread half the potatoes in the casserole, cover them with half the cod and then half the onions. Repeat the layers with the rest of the potatoes, cod and onions and pour the remaining ½ cup of oil over the top. Bake in the middle of the oven for 20 minutes, or until the top is lightly brown. Garnish the top with the olives and egg slices and sprinkle with parsley. Serve the *bacalhau* from the casserole accompanied by cruets of oil and vinegar, and a pepper mill, or a dish of freshly ground black pepper.

## Meia Desfeita de Bacalhau

SALT COD WITH CHICK-PEAS, HARD-COOKED EGGS AND BLACK OLIVES

To serve 6

1½ pounds salt cod

½ cup dried chick-peas (garbanzos),
   or substitute ¾ cup canned chick-
   peas

¾ cup olive oil

3 large onions, peeled and cut
   crosswise into ⅛ inch slices

1 cup finely chopped parsley

½ cup white wine vinegar

1 teaspoon finely chopped garlic

¼ teaspoon crushed dried hot red
   pepper

1 teaspoon salt

4 hard-cooked eggs, sliced crosswise
   into ½-inch-thick rounds

18 pitted black olives

4 to 6 parsley sprigs

Starting a day ahead, place the cod in a glass, enameled or stainless-steel pan or bowl, cover it with cold water and soak for at least 12 hours, changing the water 3 or 4 times. Wash the chick-peas in a sieve under cold running water, then place them in a heavy 2- to 3-quart saucepan and add enough cold water to cover them by 2 inches. Soak at room temperature for at least 12 hours. Bring the chick-peas to a boil over high heat, reduce the heat to low and simmer partially covered for about 2 to 2½ hours, or until the peas are tender but still intact. Replenish the liquid with boiling water from time to time if necessary. (Canned chick-peas need only be drained and rinsed under cold running water.)

Drain the cod, rinse under cold running water, place it in a saucepan and add enough fresh water to cover the fish by 1 inch. Bring to a boil over high heat. (Taste the water. If it seems excessively salty, drain, cover with fresh water, and bring to a boil again.) Reduce the heat to low and simmer un-covered for about 20 minutes, or until the fish flakes easily when prodded gently with a fork. Drain thoroughly. With a small knife, remove and dis-card any skin and bones and separate the fish into coarse flakes. Set aside.

In a heavy 10- to 12-inch skillet, heat the oil over moderate heat until a light haze forms above it. Add the onions. Stirring frequently, cook them for 5 to 8 minutes, or until lightly brown. Stir in the cod and cook for 2 min-utes longer. Then add the thoroughly drained chick-peas, chopped parsley, vinegar, garlic, red pepper and salt. Cook for 1 or 2 minutes, gently stir in the sliced eggs and continue to cook until the eggs are heated through. Taste for seasoning and transfer the mixture to a large heated platter. Scatter the olives over the cod, arrange the parsley sprigs around the platter, and serve at once, accompanied by cruets of olive oil and vinegar.

# Bacalhau Dourado

COD WITH EGGS AND GOLDEN FRIED POTATOES

To serve 4

| | |
|---|---|
| 1 pound salt cod | ½ cup olive oil |
| Vegetable oil or shortening for deep frying | ¾ cup finely chopped onions |
| | 6 eggs |
| 3 medium-sized potatoes, peeled and cut lengthwise into ⅛-by-⅛-by-2-inch strips | ½ teaspoon freshly ground black pepper |
| | 2 tablespoons finely chopped parsley |

Starting a day ahead, place the cod in a glass, enameled or stainless-steel bowl or pan, cover it with cold water and soak for at least 12 hours, changing the water 3 or 4 times.

Preheat the oven to 200°. Heat 3 or 4 inches of vegetable oil or shortening in a deep-fat fryer to 375° on a deep-frying thermometer. Line a large shallow baking pan with a double thickness of paper towels. Then deep-fry the potatoes, turning them about in the hot oil with a slotted spoon, for 2 to 3 minutes, or until they are crisp and light brown. Transfer the potatoes to the baking pan and keep them warm in the oven.

Drain the cod, rinse under cold running water, place it in a saucepan and add enough fresh water to cover the fish by 1 inch. Bring to a boil over high heat. (Taste the water. If it seems excessively salty, drain, cover with fresh water, and bring to a boil again.) Reduce the heat to low and simmer uncovered for about 20 minutes, or until the fish flakes easily when prodded gently with a fork. Drain thoroughly. With a small knife, remove and discard any skin and bones and separate the fish into coarse flakes. Return the fish to the pan, cover, and set aside.

In a heavy 10- to 12-inch skillet, heat the ½ cup of olive oil over moderate heat until a light haze forms above it. Add the onions and cook, stirring frequently, for 5 to 8 minutes, or until they are lightly brown. Stir in the cod and continue to cook, stirring, until it is heated through. With a fork or whisk, beat the eggs with the black pepper until frothy. Pour the eggs into the skillet, adding 1 or 2 tablespoons of oil if necessary. Cook over low heat, stirring with the flat of a table fork or a rubber spatula, until they form soft, creamy curds. Quickly fold in the potatoes, taste for seasoning and transfer the entire contents of the pan to a heated platter. Sprinkle with the parsley and serve at once.

## Bacalhau Trás-os-Montes
BAKED COD WITH HAM, TOMATO AND BLACK OLIVES

To serve 4

4 slices of salt cod, each about ½ inch thick (1½ pounds)
2 cups milk
⅓ cup olive oil
12 slices *presunto* cut ⅛ inch thick, or substitute 12 slices *serrano*, prosciutto or other lean smoked ham
4 slices tomato, cut about ¼ inch thick
2 hard-cooked egg yolks, sieved
¼ cup pitted black olives, cut lengthwise into ¼-inch wedges
2 teaspoons finely chopped parsley

Starting a day ahead, place the cod in a glass, enameled or stainless-steel pan or bowl, cover it with cold water and soak for at least 12 hours, changing the water 3 or 4 times.

Drain the cod, and rinse under cold running water. With a small knife, remove and discard any skin and bones, and arrange the slices in a baking dish just large enough to hold them in one layer. Warm the milk over moderate heat until bubbles begin to form around the edges of the pan. Pour it over the cod, and let it stand for 1 hour. Then drain and discard the milk.

Preheat the oven to 350°. Pour the olive oil evenly over the fish and bake in the middle of the oven for 15 minutes, basting occasionally with the oil. Place 3 slices of ham and then a slice of tomato on top of each slice of fish, baste thoroughly with the cooking liquid and bake 5 minutes longer. Sprinkle the fish with the sieved egg yolks, olive wedges and parsley and serve at once directly from the baking dish.


## Besugo al Horno
RED SNAPPER BAKED WITH POTATOES

To serve 4 to 6

2 two-pound red snappers, cleaned but with heads and tails left on, or substitute any firm white fish
1½ teaspoons salt
1 lemon, cut into 6 wedges
2 small black olives
¾ cup soft crumbs made from French or Italian bread, pulverized
in a blender or with a fork
1 teaspoon finely chopped garlic
1 tablespoon finely chopped parsley
2 tablespoons paprika
3 medium-sized boiling potatoes, peeled and cut into ¼-inch rounds
Freshly ground black pepper
1 cup water
½ cup olive oil

Preheat the oven to 350°. Wash the fish under cold running water and pat them dry, inside and out, with paper towels. Sprinkle the fish with 1 teaspoon of the salt, then place them side by side on a board or plate.

With a small, sharp knife, score each fish, by making three crosswise parallel cuts about ¼ inch deep, 2 inches long and 1½ inches apart. Insert a wedge of lemon skin side up in each cut. Insert a black olive in the exposed eye socket of each fish.

In a small bowl, combine the bread crumbs, garlic, parsley and paprika. Spread the potato slices evenly on the bottom of a 16-by-10-by-2-inch baking-serving dish. Sprinkle them with the remaining ½ teaspoon of salt and a few grindings of pepper and place the fish side by side on top. Pour the water down the side of the baking dish and pour the olive oil over the fish. Sprinkle them evenly with the bread-crumb mixture.

Bake in the middle of the oven for 30 minutes, or until the fish feels firm when pressed lightly with a finger and the potatoes beneath them are done. Serve at once, directly from the baking dish.

## Escabeche

FISH PICKLED WITH CARROTS, ONIONS AND BAY LEAVES

To serve 4 to 6 as a main course or
 6 to 8 as a first course

⅓ cup plus ¾ cup olive oil

2 pounds halibut steaks, cut about
 ¾ inch thick

2 large onions, peeled, cut into ⅛-
 inch slices and separated into rings

4 medium-sized carrots, scraped and
 coarsely grated

1 cup white wine vinegar

2 large bay leaves, crumbled

2 teaspoons finely chopped garlic

2 teaspoons salt

¼ teaspoon crushed dried hot red
 pepper

¼ teaspoon freshly ground black
 pepper

In a heavy 10- to 12-inch skillet, heat ⅓ cup of the olive oil over moderate heat until a light haze forms above it. Add the fish steaks and cook them for 4 or 5 minutes on each side, turning them with a large spatula. When they are a golden brown, transfer them to paper towels to drain and cool.

In a clean 10- to 12-inch skillet, heat the remaining ¾ cup of oil over moderate heat until a light haze forms above it. Add the onion rings and, stirring frequently, cook for 5 minutes or until they are soft and transparent but not brown. Stir in the carrots, vinegar, bay leaf, garlic, salt and red and black pepper and cook for 5 minutes longer, stirring occasionally. Taste for seasoning.

Remove the skin and any bones from the fish. Spread a cup or so of the hot marinade evenly in a glass or enamel dish about 6 inches in diameter and 4 inches deep. Arrange half the fish on top, cover it with a cup of marinade, add the remaining fish and spread the remaining marinade over it.

Cover tightly with foil or plastic wrap and marinate in the refrigerator for at least 2 days. Serve the *escabeche* from the dish in which it has marinated.

# Mero en Salsa Verde

POLLOCK IN GREEN SAUCE

To serve 6

3 pounds pollock steaks, each cut
   ½ inch thick, or substitute halibut
   or other firm white fish steaks cut
   ½ inch thick
½ cup plus 3 tablespoons flour
⅓ cup olive oil
⅓ cup finely chopped onions

2 cups water
⅓ cup dry white wine
1 teaspoon finely chopped garlic
⅓ cup finely chopped parsley
1½ teaspoons salt
2 tablespoons cooked fresh green
   peas or thoroughly defrosted
   frozen peas (optional)

With a small, sharp knife, remove the skin from each steak, and pat the steaks dry with paper towels. Sprinkle them with salt, then dip the steaks in the ½ cup of flour, and shake them vigorously to remove the excess flour.

In a heavy 12-inch skillet, heat the olive oil over moderate heat until a light haze forms above it. Add the fish and cook for about 4 minutes on each side, turning them with tongs and regulating the heat so that they color evenly without burning. Remove the pan from the heat and with a bulb baster transfer the oil remaining in the pan to a heavy 6- to 8-inch skillet. Cover the fish steaks in the pan to keep them warm while you prepare the sauce.

Heat the oil again until a light haze forms above it. Add the onions and, stirring constantly, cook for about 5 minutes, or until they are soft and transparent but not brown. Stir in the 3 tablespoons of flour, mix thoroughly and pour in the water and wine. Cook over high heat, stirring constantly with a whisk until the sauce comes to a boil and thickens lightly. Reduce the heat to low and simmer for about 3 minutes.

Meanwhile, with a mortar and pestle or the back of a large spoon, mash the garlic, parsley and salt to a smooth paste. Thin it with about ¼ cup of the simmering sauce, then whisk it into the remaining sauce. Cook, stirring constantly, for a minute or so. Taste for seasoning.

Scatter the peas, if you are using them, on top of the fish steaks, pour the sauce over them and cook uncovered over low heat for about 3 minutes, basting occasionally until the fish and peas are just heated through. Serve at once on a large heated platter.

## Merluza a la Gallega
POACHED HAKE WITH POTATOES AND TOMATO SAUCE

To serve 4

12 small firm boiling-type potatoes, each about 1½ inches in diameter, peeled
1 small onion, peeled and cut in half
1 small bay leaf
1½ pounds of hake, haddock or cod fillets
6 tablespoons olive oil

6 medium-sized garlic cloves, peeled and gently bruised with the flat of a knife
3 medium-sized tomatoes, peeled, seeded and coarsely chopped (*huevos a la flamenca, page 68*)
½ teaspoon salt
1 tablespoon paprika
1 teaspoon red wine vinegar

In a heavy 12-inch skillet at least 2 inches deep, bring 2 quarts of water to a boil over high heat. Drop in the potatoes, onion, and bay leaf. There should be enough water to cover them completely; if necessary, add more. Boil briskly uncovered until the potatoes are tender but not falling apart. With a slotted spoon, transfer the potatoes to a plate. Add the fish fillets to the liquid remaining in the pan and reduce the heat to low. Cover the skillet tightly and simmer for 8 to 10 minutes, or until the fish flakes easily when prodded gently with a fork.

Meanwhile, heat the oil in a heavy 8- to 10-inch skillet over moderate heat until a light haze forms above it. Add the garlic cloves and, stirring frequently, cook them for about 5 minutes, or until light brown. With a slotted spoon, remove and discard them, then add the tomatoes and salt. Cook briskly, stirring and mashing the tomatoes with a large spoon, until the mixture is thick enough to hold its shape almost solidly in the spoon. Stir in the paprika and set aside.

Pour off all but 1 cup of liquid from the fish, discard the onion and bay leaf and return the potatoes to the skillet. With the back of a spoon, force the tomato mixture through a fine sieve, directly over the fish. Simmer over low heat for 5 minutes, basting the fish and potatoes frequently with the sauce. Sprinkle with the vinegar and serve at once, directly from the skillet or from a deep heated platter.

# Merluza al Horno

HAKE BAKED WITH SLICED POTATOES AND TOMATO SAUCE

To serve 4

6 tablespoons olive oil
½ cup finely chopped onions
3 medium-sized tomatoes, peeled,
  seeded and finely chopped (*see*
  *huevos a la flamenca, page 68*), or
  substitute 1 cup chopped, drained,
  canned tomatoes
1 large firm boiling-type potato,
  peeled and sliced crosswise into
  ⅛-inch-thick rounds

Salt
2 pounds hake, haddock, or cod
  fillets
2 tablespoons fresh lemon juice
½ cup water
¼ cup soft fresh crumbs made from
  French or Italian bread, trimmed
  of crusts and pulverized in a
  blender or torn apart with a fork
2 teaspoons finely chopped parsley

In a heavy 8- to 10-inch skillet, heat 2 tablespoons of the oil over moderate heat until a light haze forms above it. Add the onions and, stirring frequently, cook for 8 to 10 minutes, or until they are soft and lightly browned. Add the tomatoes, and continue cooking for 10 to 15 minutes, stirring and mashing the tomatoes with a large spoon, until the mixture is thick enough to hold its shape almost solidly in the spoon.

Preheat the oven to 350°. With a pastry brush and 1 tablespoon olive oil, coat the bottom and sides of an 8-by-10-by-2-inch baking dish. In it arrange the potato slices in a single layer, overlapping them slightly, and sprinkle them lightly with salt. Arrange the fish fillets side by side on top of the potatoes, sprinkle them liberally with salt, 2 tablespoons each of lemon juice and oil and spread with the tomato mixture. Pour the water in at the side of the dish. Mix the bread crumbs with parsley and scatter the mixture over the top of the fish. Sprinkle with the remaining tablespoon of oil.

Bring to a simmer on top of the stove. Then lay a piece of foil or wax paper loosely over the dish and bake in the middle of the oven for 20 to 25 minutes, or until the fillets flake easily when prodded gently with a fork and the potatoes are tender. Serve at once, directly from the casserole.

# Merluza Marinera

POACHED HAKE FILLETS WITH TOMATO AND ALMOND SAUCE

To serve 4

¼ cup olive oil
½ cup finely chopped onions
1 tablespoon finely chopped garlic
⅓ cup blanched almonds, pulverized in a blender or with a nut grinder or mortar and pestle
¼ cup coarsely crumbled French or Italian bread, trimmed of all crusts
4 medium-sized tomatoes, peeled, seeded and finely chopped *(see*

*huevos a la flamenca, page 68)*, or substitute 1½ cups chopped, drained, canned tomatoes
4 teaspoons fresh lemon juice
1 teaspoon salt
2 pounds hake, haddock or cod fillets
¼ cup slivered and lightly toasted blanched almonds *(see romescu, page 79)*
2 tablespoons finely chopped parsley

To make the *sofrito,* heat the olive oil over moderate heat in a heavy 8- to 10-inch skillet until a light haze forms above it. Add the onions and garlic and, stirring frequently, cook for 5 minutes, or until the onions are soft and transparent but not brown. Add the almonds and bread, stir for a minute or so, then add the tomatoes. Raise the heat and cook briskly, uncovered, until most of the liquid in the pan evaporates and the mixture is thick enough to hold its shape almost solidly in a spoon.

In a heavy 10- to 12-inch skillet, bring 6 cups of water, 3 teaspoons of the fresh lemon juice and the 1 teaspoon of salt to a boil over high heat. Reduce the heat to low, add the fish steaks and simmer uncovered for 5 to 8 minutes, or until the fish flakes easily when it is prodded gently with a fork.

With a slotted spatula, transfer the fish to a heated serving platter. Bring the *sofrito* to a boil over moderate heat, stir in the remaining teaspoon of lemon juice and add up to ½ cup of the fish stock, 1 or 2 tablespoons at a time. The *sofrito* should be just thick enough to coat the spoon lightly. Taste for seasoning. Pour the sauce over the fish, garnish with slivered almonds and parsley, and serve at once.

## Zarzuela de Mariscos

CATALONIAN SHELLFISH STEW

To serve 6

A 1½ pound live lobster
12 large raw shrimp, in their shells
¼ cup olive oil
1 cup finely chopped onions
1 tablespoon finely chopped garlic
2 small sweet red or green peppers,
  deribbed, seeded and finely
  chopped
2 tablespoons finely chopped *serrano*
  ham, or substitute prosciutto or
  other lean smoked ham
6 medium-sized tomatoes, peeled,
  seeded and finely chopped (*see
  huevos a la flamenca, page 68*)
½ cup blanched almonds, pulverized

in a blender or with a nut grinder
  or mortar and pestle
1 large bay leaf, crumbled
⅛ teaspoon ground saffron or saffron
  threads crushed with a mortar and
  pestle or with the back of a spoon
1 teaspoon salt
Freshly ground black pepper
3 cups water
½ cup dry white wine
1 tablespoon fresh lemon juice
12 mussels, washed, scrubbed and
  with black tufts removed
12 small clams, washed and
  thoroughly scrubbed
½ pound sea scallops, cut in half

With a cleaver or large, heavy knife, chop off the tail section of the lobster at the point where it joins the body. Then cut the tail crosswise into 1-inch-thick slices. Twist or cut off the large claws, and cut the body of the lobster in half lengthwise. Remove and discard the gelatinous sac (stomach) in the head and the long white intestinal vein which is attached to it, but leave the greenish brown tomalley (liver) and the black coral (roe) if there is any.

Shell the shrimp but leave the tail shell attached. With a small, sharp knife, devein them by making a shallow incision down their backs and lifting out the intestinal vein with the point of the knife. Set the lobster and shrimp aside.

In a heavy 6- to 8-quart casserole, heat the olive oil over moderate heat until a light haze forms above it. Add the onions, garlic, and red or green peppers and, stirring frequently, cook for 5 minutes, or until the vegetables are soft but not brown.

Stir in the ham and cook for a minute or two. Then add the tomatoes, pulverized almonds, bay leaf, saffron, salt and a few grindings of pepper, raise the heat and bring to a boil. Cook briskly for about 5 minutes, or until most of the liquid in the pan evaporates and the mixture is thick enough to hold its shape lightly in a spoon.

Add the water, wine and lemon juice and bring to a boil. Stir thoroughly, then drop in the lobster, mussels and clams. Cover the casserole tightly, reduce the heat to moderate and cook for 10 minutes. Add the shrimp and scallops, cover, and cook 5 minutes longer. Discard any clams or mussels that have not opened.

Taste the *zarzuela* for seasoning and serve it directly from the casserole, sprinkled with parsley if you like.

## *Amêijoas na Cataplana*
STEAMED CLAMS WITH SAUSAGES, HAM, TOMATOES AND SPICES

To serve 4 as a main course, 6 as a
    first course

½ pound *linguiça* sausage or
    substitute *chorizo* or other garlic-
    seasoned smoked pork sausage
½ cup olive oil
4 medium-sized onions, thinly sliced
1 teaspoon paprika
¼ teaspoon crushed hot dried red
    pepper
Freshly ground black pepper
¼ pound *presunto* ham, finely
    chopped, or substitute prosciutto
    or other lean smoked ham
2 medium-sized tomatoes, peeled,
    seeded and coarsely chopped *(see
    huevos a la flamenca, page 68)*
½ cup finely chopped parsley
½ cup dry white wine
1 tablespoon finely chopped garlic
2 small bay leaves, crumbled
36 small hard-shelled clams, washed
    and thoroughly scrubbed

With a small, sharp knife, remove the casings of the sausages. Crumble the meat coarsely and drop it into a sieve. Plunge the sieve into a pan of boiling water and boil briskly for 1 minute. Then spread the sausage meat out on a double thickness of paper towels to drain.

In a heavy 12-inch skillet or similar-sized casserole, heat the olive oil over moderate heat until a light haze forms above it. Add the onions and, stirring frequently, cook for 5 minutes, or until they are soft and transparent but not brown. Add the paprika, red pepper and a liberal grinding of black pepper and cook for a minute or two. Then add the sausage meat, ham, tomatoes, parsley, wine, garlic and bay leaves, raise the heat and bring to a boil. Stirring constantly, cook briskly until most of the liquid in the pan evaporates.

Arrange the clams hinged side down over the meat and tomato mixture, cover the skillet tightly and cook over moderate heat for about 10 minutes, or until all the clams open. Discard any that remain closed. To serve, transfer the clams to heated soup plates and ladle the sauce over them.

NOTE: This dish takes its name from the Portuguese *cataplana*, a metal casserole shaped like a clam.

## Salpicón de Mariscos

SHRIMP AND LOBSTER SALAD

To serve 6

1 large onion, peeled and cut into
   quarters
¼ cup wine vinegar

1 teaspoon olive oil
1 large bay leaf
1 tablespoon salt
1½ pounds raw shrimp, in their shells
A 1½- to 2-pound live lobster

In a 6- to 8-quart casserole, combine the quartered onion, vinegar, 1 teaspoon olive oil, bay leaf and 1 tablespoon of salt with 2 quarts of water.
Bring to a boil over high heat, drop in the shrimp and reduce the heat to
low. Simmer uncovered for 3 or 4 minutes or until the shrimp turn pink.
Then remove them with a slotted spoon and set the shrimp aside.

Bring the liquid remaining in the casserole to a boil again. Plunge the lobster head first into the liquid, cover and boil briskly for 10 to 15 minutes or
until the shell turns bright red. Remove the lobster to a plate and let it cool.

Shell the shrimp. Devein them by making a shallow incision down their
backs with a small, sharp knife, and lifting out their intestinal veins with the
point of the knife. Cut the shrimp into ½-inch dice.

Twist off the large claws of the lobster at the point where they meet the
body and crack each claw in two or three places with a nutcracker. Split the
lobster in half and remove all of the meat from the claws, body and tail. Remove and save the greenish brown tomalley (liver) and the red coral (roe).
Cut the lobster into ½-inch dice and refrigerate the lobster and shrimp for
at least 1 hour or until thoroughly chilled.

MAYONNAISE
2 egg yolks
3 teaspoons lemon juice
½ teaspoon salt

¼ teaspoon white pepper
1 cup olive oil
3 tablespoons white wine vinegar
1 tablespoon finely chopped parsley

To make the mayonnaise, warm a large mixing bowl in hot water, dry it
quickly but thoroughly, and drop in the egg yolks. With a whisk, or a rotary or electric beater, beat the yolks vigorously for about 2 minutes until
they thicken and cling to the beater. Add a teaspoon of the lemon juice, ½ teaspoon of salt and the white pepper. Then beat in ½ cup of the oil, ½ teaspoon at a time; make sure each addition is absorbed before adding more.
By the time ½ cup of oil has been beaten in, the sauce should be the consistency of very thick cream.

Pour in the remaining oil in a slow, thin stream, beating constantly. Beat
in the remaining 2 teaspoons of lemon juice, the vinegar and parsley. With
the back of a spoon, force the lobster tomalley and coral (if any) through a
fine sieve into the mayonnaise. Mix thoroughly and taste for seasoning.

1½ cups finely chopped crisp lettuce, preferably romaine
1 medium-sized tomato, peeled, seeded and finely chopped (see *huevos a la flamenca, page 68*)

½ cup finely chopped onions
2 hard-cooked eggs, the yolks forced through a sieve and the whites separated and finely chopped

Just before serving, toss the shrimp, lobster, lettuce, tomato, chopped onions and sieved egg yolks together thoroughly in a large chilled bowl. Add about ½ cup of the mayonnaise and turn the shellfish and vegetables about with a spoon to coat them evenly. Garnish the salad with chopped egg whites and serve the remaining mayonnaise separately in a sauceboat.

## Almejas a la Marinera
CLAMS IN WHITE WINE WITH GARLIC, ONIONS AND TOMATOES

To serve 2 as a main course, 4 as a first course

3 tablespoons olive oil
½ cup finely chopped onions
1 teaspoon finely chopped garlic
2 tablespoons coarsely crumbled white bread, trimmed of crusts
½ cup peeled, seeded and finely chopped tomatoes (see *huevos a la flamenca, page 68*)

1 hard-cooked egg, the yolk sieved and the white finely chopped
2 dozen small hard-shell clams, washed and thoroughly scrubbed
1 cup dry white wine
Salt
Freshly ground black pepper
2 tablespoons finely chopped parsley
1 lemon, cut into 6 or 8 wedges

To make the *sofrito*, heat the oil in a heavy 8- to 10-inch skillet, until a light haze forms above it. Add the onions and garlic. Stirring frequently, cook for 5 minutes or until the onions are soft and transparent but not brown.

Stir in the bread, tomatoes and sieved egg yolk. Cook for about 5 minutes, mashing and stirring with a spoon until most of the liquid in the pan evaporates and the mixture becomes a thick, smooth purée. Set aside.

Place the clams hinged side down in a heavy 10- to 12-inch skillet, pour in the wine and bring to a boil over high heat. Cover tightly, reduce the heat to low, and steam for 8 to 10 minutes or until the clams open. With tongs or a slotted spoon, remove the clams from the skillet and place them on a deep heated platter. Discard any clams that remain closed.

Strain the liquid in the skillet through a sieve directly into the *sofrito*. Bring to a boil, stirring; taste and season with salt and pepper.

Pour the sauce over the clams, sprinkle the top with the egg white and parsley and garnish the platter with the lemon wedges. Serve at once.

## Mariscos a la Costa Brava

SHELLFISH IN SPICED TOMATO SAUCE

To serve 6

SAUCE
¼ cup olive oil
1 cup finely chopped onions
2 tablespoons finely chopped garlic
9 medium-sized tomatoes, peeled, seeded and finely chopped (*see huevos a la flamenca, page 68*), or substitute 3 cups chopped, drained, canned tomatoes
2 tablespoons tomato paste
A 2-ounce can flat anchovy fillets, coarsely chopped
1 large bay leaf
1 teaspoon oregano, crumbled
¼ teaspoon basil, crumbled
⅛ teaspoon cayenne pepper
1 teaspoon salt
¼ teaspoon freshly ground black pepper
1 cup water
¾ cup dry white wine
2 tablespoons fresh lemon juice
2 tablespoons finely chopped parsley

In a heavy 6- to 8-quart casserole, heat ¼ cup of the olive oil over moderate heat until a light haze forms above it. Add the onions and garlic and, stirring frequently, cook for 5 minutes, or until the onions are soft and transparent but not brown. Stir in the tomatoes, tomato paste, anchovy fillets, bay leaf, oregano, basil, cayenne pepper, salt and black pepper and raise the heat. Stirring and mashing the tomatoes with a large spoon, cook briskly until most of the liquid in the pan evaporates and the mixture is thick enough to hold its shape lightly in the spoon. Stir in the water, wine, lemon juice and parsley. Set the casserole aside.

SHELLFISH
A 1½ pound live lobster
1 pound raw medium-sized shrimp, in their shells
¼ cup olive oil
½ pound sea scallops, cut in half
12 small hard-shelled clams, washed and thoroughly scrubbed
12 mussels, washed and thoroughly scrubbed and with black, ropelike tufts removed

With a cleaver or large, heavy knife, chop off the tail section of the lobster at the point where it joins the body, and cut the tail crosswise into 1-inch-thick slices. Twist or cut off the claws, cut the body in half lengthwise and then crosswise into quarters. Remove and discard the gelatinous sac (stomach) in the head and the long white intestinal vein attached to it.

Shell the shrimp but leave the tail shells attached. With a small, sharp knife, devein the shrimp by making a shallow incision down their backs and lifting out the intestinal vein with the point of the knife. Wash the shrimp under cold running water, and drain thoroughly.

In a heavy 10- to 12-inch skillet, heat the remaining ¼ cup of olive oil over moderate heat until a light haze forms above it. Add the lobster. Turning the pieces with tongs, cook for 3 to 4 minutes until the shells begin to turn pink. Transfer the lobster to paper towels to drain. Add the shrimp and scallops to the pan and cook, stirring for 1 or 2 minutes until the scallops are somewhat firm and the shrimp turn pink. Drain on paper towels.

Add the lobster, clams and mussels to the casserole, turning them about with a spoon to coat them evenly with the sauce. Then bring to a boil over high heat, reduce the heat to moderate and cover tightly. After 10 minutes, add the shrimp and scallops, cover again, and cook for 5 minutes longer. Discard any clams or mussels that have not opened. Taste for seasoning and serve at once, directly from the casserole.

## Marmita-kua
FRESH TUNA AND POTATO STEW

To serve 2

| | |
|---|---|
| ¼ cup olive oil | ¼-inch-thick rounds |
| 1 cup finely chopped onions | ¼ teaspoon paprika |
| 1 teaspoon finely chopped garlic | 2 teaspoons salt |
| | ¼ teaspoon freshly ground black pepper |
| 3 medium-sized tomatoes, peeled and finely chopped, (see huevos a la flamenca, page 68), or substitute 1 cup chopped, drained, canned tomatoes | 2 cups boiling water |
| | 1 pound fresh tuna or halibut, sliced 1 inch thick and cut into pieces 1 inch wide and 2 inches long |
| 3 medium-sized firm boiling-type potatoes, peeled and sliced into | 1 cup coarsely crumbled French or Italian bread |

In a heavy 3- to 4-quart casserole, heat the olive oil over moderate heat until a light haze forms above it. Add the onions and garlic and cook, stirring occasionally, for 5 to 8 minutes or until the onions are lightly colored. Add the tomatoes, raise the heat and cook briskly, stirring frequently, until most of the liquid in the pan evaporates and the mixture is thick enough to hold its shape lightly in a spoon.

Add the potatoes, and turn them about with a spoon until they are evenly coated with the tomato mixture. Sprinkle with the paprika, salt, pepper and pour in the boiling water. The liquid should completely cover the potatoes; add more water if necessary. Bring to a boil over high heat, cover tightly, reduce the heat to low and simmer for about 15 minutes, or until the potatoes are barely tender. Stir in the fish, cover again and cook for 5 minutes, or until the potatoes are tender and the fish flakes easily. Do not overcook. Taste for seasoning, then sprinkle the bread over the top, but do not stir it into the stew. Cover and cook over the lowest possible heat for 3 or 4 minutes. Serve at once directly from the casserole.

## Changurro

CRABMEAT WITH SHERRY AND BRANDY

To serve 4 as a main course or 6 as
  a first course

8 tablespoons butter
1 tablespoon olive oil
1 large garlic clove, peeled and cut
  lengthwise in half
1 cup finely chopped onions
¾ cup finely chopped leeks, white
  part only
1 small tomato, peeled, seeded and
  coarsely chopped *(see huevos a la
  flamenca, page 68)*, or substitute
  ¼ cup chopped, drained, canned
  tomatoes
3 tablespoons pale dry sherry
3 tablespoons brandy

1 pound fresh crabmeat or two 7½-
  ounce cans crabmeat, drained and
  all bits of shell and cartilage
  removed
3 tablespoons chicken stock, fresh
  or canned
3 tablespoons finely chopped parsley
A pinch of cayenne pepper
½ teaspoon salt
¼ teaspoon freshly ground black
  pepper
1 cup fresh soft crumbs made from
  French or Italian bread, trimmed
  of crusts and pulverized in a
  blender or shredded with a fork

In a heavy 10- to 12-inch skillet, melt 4 tablespoons of the butter in the oil over moderate heat. When the foam begins to subside, add the garlic and, stirring constantly, cook for a minute or two until lightly browned, then with a slotted spoon, remove and discard it. Add the onions and leeks and cook, stirring frequently, for about 5 minutes, or until they are soft and transparent but not brown. Stir in the tomato, sherry and brandy, raise the heat and bring to a boil. Stirring almost constantly, cook briskly for about 5 minutes, or until almost all the liquid has evaporated and the mixture is thick enough to hold its shape lightly in a spoon.

Reduce the heat to low, stir in the crabmeat, chicken stock, 2 tablespoons of the parsley, the cayenne, salt and black pepper and simmer uncovered for 3 minutes. Taste for seasoning and set aside.

Preheat the oven to 350°. In a 6- to 8-inch skillet, melt the remaining 4 tablespoons of butter over moderate heat. When the foam begins to subside, stir in the crumbs and the remaining tablespoon of parsley and cook, stirring constantly, until all of the butter has been absorbed and the crumbs have begun to separate and color lightly. Set aside.

To assemble the *changurro,* spoon the crabmeat mixture into individual scallop shells or ramekins, dividing it equally among them, or spread it evenly in a baking dish about 6 inches in diameter and 4 inches deep. Sprinkle with the crumb mixture and bake in the middle of the oven for about 15 minutes, or until the crumbs are crisp and a golden brown. Serve at once.

## Truchas a la Navarra

MARINATED TROUT BAKED WITH RED WINE AND HERBS

To serve 4

½ cup dry red wine
¼ cup olive oil
¼ cup water
½ cup finely chopped onions
1 tablespoon finely cut fresh mint
  or ½ teaspoon crumbled dried
  mint

½ teaspoon dried rosemary
½ teaspoon dried thyme
1 small bay leaf, crumbled
15 to 20 whole black peppercorns
1 teaspoon salt
4 trout, 8 to 12 ounces each, cleaned
  but with heads and tails left on
3 egg yolks, lightly beaten

In a flameproof glass, enamel or stainless-steel baking dish large enough to hold the fish in one layer, combine the red wine, olive oil, water, onions, mint, rosemary, thyme, bay leaf, peppercorns and salt, and stir thoroughly. Wash the trout under cold running water and dry them completely with paper towels. Then place them in the marinade, turning them about to coat them thoroughly. Marinate at room temperature for about 30 minutes, turning the trout over after 15 minutes.

Preheat the oven to 350°. On top of the stove bring the marinade to a simmer, then lay a sheet of wax paper or foil lightly over the baking dish. Bake in the middle of the oven for 20 minutes, or until the fish is firm to the touch. Be careful not to overcook.

With a slotted spatula, transfer the fish to a heated serving platter and cover loosely with foil to keep them warm. Strain the cooking liquid through a fine sieve into a small saucepan, pressing down hard on the onions and herbs with the back of a spoon before discarding them. Whisk about ¼ cup of the liquid into the beaten egg yolks, then whisk the mixture into the remaining liquid in the pan. Heat slowly, whisking constantly, until the sauce thickens lightly. (Do not let it come anywhere near a boil or it will curdle.) Taste for seasoning.

Pour the sauce over the trout or serve the sauce separately. Traditionally the trout are accompanied by hot, freshly boiled potatoes.

# Paella

SAFFRON RICE WITH SEAFOOD AND CHICKEN

To serve 6

A 1½- to 2-pound live lobster
6 medium-sized raw shrimps in their
  shells
6 small hard-shelled clams
6 mussels
3 *chorizos,* or substitute ½ pound
  other garlic-seasoned smoked
  pork sausage
A 1½- to 2-pound chicken, cut into
  12 serving pieces
2 teaspoons salt
Freshly ground black pepper
½ cup olive oil
2 ounces lean boneless pork, cut
  into ¼-inch cubes
½ cup finely chopped onions
1 teaspoon finely chopped garlic

1 medium-sized sweet red or green
  pepper, seeded, deribbed and cut
  into strips 1½ inches long and ¼
  inch wide
1 large tomato, peeled, seeded and
  finely chopped *(see huevos a la
  flamenca, page 68)*
3 cups raw medium or long-grain
  regular-milled rice or imported
  short-grain rice
¼ teaspoon ground saffron or saffron
  threads pulverized with a mortar and
  pestle or with the back of a spoon
6 cups boiling water
½ cup fresh peas (½ pound) or
  substitute ½ cup thoroughly
  defrosted frozen peas
2 lemons, each cut lengthwise into
  6 wedges

NOTE: In Spain, a *paella* may be simple or elaborate. Vary the combination of chicken, meats and shellfish, if you like, to suit your taste. For example, you may omit the lobster altogether or replace it with 6 or 8 additional shrimp. Clams and mussels may be used interchangeably. Add rabbit or let it replace the chicken. Cubed ham, veal, or beef might be used instead of the pork or the sausage. Squid—even snails—are appropriate. Cooked green string beans or artichoke hearts may be added, or substituted for the peas.

With a cleaver or large, heavy knife, chop off the tail section of the lobster at the point where it joins the body and twist or cut off the large claws. Remove and discard the gelatinous sac (stomach) in the head and the long intestinal vein attached to it. Without removing the shell, cut the tail crosswise into 1-inch-thick slices and split the body of the lobster in half lengthwise, then crosswise into quarters. Set aside.

Shell the shrimp, leaving the tails intact. With a small, sharp knife, devein the shrimp by making a shallow incision down their backs and lifting out the intestinal vein with the point of the knife. Scrub the clams and mussels thoroughly with a stiff brush or soapless steel-mesh scouring pad under cold running water and remove the black, ropelike tufts from the mussels. Set the shrimp, clams and mussels aside on separate plates.

Place the sausages in an 8- to 10-inch skillet and prick them in two or three places with the point of a small, sharp knife. Add enough cold water to cover them completely and bring to a boil over high heat. Then reduce the heat to low and simmer uncovered for 5 minutes. Drain on paper towels and slice them into ¼-inch rounds.

Pat the chicken dry with paper towels and season it with 1 teaspoon of the salt and a few gridings of pepper. In a heavy 10- to 12-inch skillet, heat ¼ cup of the olive oil over high heat until a light haze forms above it. Add the chicken, skin side down, and brown it well, turning the pieces with tongs and regulating the heat so they color evenly without burning. As the pieces become a rich golden brown, remove them to a plate.

Add the lobster to the skillet. Turning the pieces frequently, cook over high heat for 2 or 3 minutes or until the shell begins to turn pink. Set the lobster aside on a separate plate and add the sausages to the pan. Brown the slices quickly on both sides, then spread them on paper towels to drain.

To make the *sofrito*, discard all the fat remaining in the skillet and in its place add the remaining ¼ cup of olive oil. Heat until a light haze forms above it, add the pork and brown it quickly on all sides over high heat. Add the onions, garlic, pepper strips and tomato. Stirring constantly, cook briskly until most of the liquid in the pan evaporates and the mixture is thick enough to hold its shape lightly in a spoon. Set the *sofrito* aside.

About a half hour before you plan to serve the *paella*, preheat the oven to 400°. In a 14-inch *paella* pan or a skillet or casserole at least 14 inches in diameter and 2- to 2½- inches deep, combine the *sofrito*, rice, the remaining 1 teaspoon of salt and the saffron. Pour in the boiling water and, stirring constantly, bring to a boil over high heat. Remove the pan from the heat immediately. (Taste the liquid for seasoning and add more salt if necessary.) Arrange the chicken, lobster, sausage, shrimp, clams and mussels on top of the rice and scatter the peas at random over the whole. Set the pan on the floor of the oven and bake uncovered for 25 to 30 minutes or until all the liquid has been absorbed by the rice and the grains are tender but not too soft. At no point should the *paella* be stirred after it goes in the oven.

When the *paella* is done, remove it from the oven and drape a kitchen towel loosely over the top. Let it rest for 5 to 8 minutes. Then garnish the *paella* with the lemons and serve at the table directly from the pan.

OUTDOOR COOKING: In Spain, *paella* is often made out-of-doors on wood fires, but a large charcoal grill serves as well. Following the recipe above, prepare the seafood, chicken, sausages and *sofrito* at the kitchen stove and have the other ingredients ready for the final assembly outside.

About an hour and a half before you plan to serve the *paella*, light a 2- to 3-inch-thick layer of coals in a charcoal broiler and let them burn until white ash appears on the surface. This may take as long as an hour. Adjust the grill to place it 2½- to 3-inches above the coals. If your grill is not absolutely flat on top or tends to tilt, remove it and use a rack from the oven large enough for its four corners to rest on the rim of the grill.

In a 14-inch *paella* pan, or a skillet or flameproof baking dish 14 inches in di-

*Continued on next page*

ameter and 2 to 2½ inches deep, combine the *sofrito,* rice, 1 teaspoon of salt and the saffron. Place the pan on the grill, pour in the boiling water, and stir the ingredients thoroughly, spreading the rice evenly over the surface of the pan. Quickly arrange the chicken, sausage and seafood on top, making sure that the clams and mussels are turned with their hinges downward. Scatter the peas over the top and let the *paella* cook briskly, uncovered and undisturbed, for 15 to 18 minutes, or until all the liquid has been absorbed by the rice. At no point after the *paella* has come to a boil should it be stirred.

When it is done, remove the *paella* from the grill and drape a kitchen towel or a large piece of aluminum foil over the top of the pan. Let the *paella* rest for 5 to 8 minutes, then remove the towel or foil, garnish with lemons and serve directly from the pan. Almost always, because of the intense heat generated by the charcoal, the rice will form a light brown crust on the bottom of the pan. The Spanish prefer it this way and generally serve the crust with the *paella;* however, should the crust char, it is best to leave it clinging to the pan and not serve it with the rest of the rice.


## Caldeirada
SEAFOOD STEW

To serve 8

1 cup finely chopped onions
½ cup green pepper, seeded, deribbed and finely chopped
3 medium-sized tomatoes, peeled, seeded and finely chopped (*see huevos a la flamenca, page 68*)
1 teaspoon finely chopped garlic
½ teaspoon salt
½ teaspoon freshly ground black pepper
24 small hard-shelled clams, washed and thoroughly scrubbed
⅔ cup olive oil

1½ pounds each of two kinds of firm, white fish, sliced 1 inch thick, boned, skinned and cut into 1½-inch cubes (halibut, haddock, bass, red snapper, cod, pollock and hake are all suitable)
1½ pounds squid, cleaned (*see calamares en su tinta, opposite*) and cut into strips 2 inches long and ½ inch wide
1½ cups dry white wine
8 slices homemade-type white bread, cut diagonally into two triangles
¼ cup finely chopped parsley


In a bowl, combine the onions, green peppers, tomatoes, garlic, salt and black pepper, tossing them about with a spoon to mix them thoroughly.

Place the clams in a heavy 5- to 6-quart casserole and pour in ⅓ cup of the olive oil. Scatter half of the vegetable mixture over the clams, and add the fish and squid. Spread the rest of the vegetable mixture on top and pour in the wine. Bring to a boil over high heat, and reduce the heat to low. Cover tightly and simmer undisturbed for 20 minutes, or until the clams open and the fish flakes easily when prodded gently with a fork. (Discard any clams that do not open.)

Meanwhile, heat the remaining ⅓ cup of oil in a 10- to 12-inch skillet, add the bread (in two batches if necessary) and brown well on both sides. Transfer to paper towels to drain.

To serve, place two triangles of bread in each of eight individual soup plates. Ladle the soup over the bread, arrange the clams, fish and squid on top and sprinkle with parsley.

## Calamares en su Tinta
SQUID IN ITS OWN INK

To serve 6

3 pounds small fresh whole squid
  with ink sacs
½ cup olive oil
1 cup finely chopped onions
1 teaspoon finely chopped garlic
¼ cup finely chopped parsley

⅛ teaspoon ground nutmeg,
  preferably freshly grated
1 teaspoon salt
¼ teaspoon freshly ground black
  pepper
1 cup cold water
2 tablespoons flour

Following the directions given in the diagrams on the next page, clean the squid and carefully reserve the ink sacs in a small fine sieve set over a bowl. Wash the tail cone, fins and tentacles under cold running water and pat them completely dry with paper towels. Then slice the tail crosswise into ½-inch-wide rings. Cut the tentacles from the base, cut the base and each tentacle into 2 or 3 pieces, and slice each fin in half.

In a heavy 10- to 12-inch skillet, heat the olive oil over high heat until a light haze forms above it. Add the squid, onions, garlic and parsley and cook briskly uncovered for 5 or 6 minutes, stirring. Add the nutmeg, salt and pepper, reduce the heat to low, cover the skillet, and simmer for 20 minutes.

Meanwhile, mash the ink sacs in the sieve with the back of a spoon and press out as much of the ink as possible. Pour the water over the sacs and mash again to extract any remaining ink. The ink is usually black but may be brown, and in either case the water should become dark and opaque. With a whisk beat the flour into the ink and continue to beat until smooth.

When the squid has simmered its allotted 20 minutes, pour the ink over it and, stirring constantly, bring to a boil over high heat. Immediately reduce the heat to its lowest point, cover and simmer for 5 minutes. Remove the pan from the heat and, without removing the cover, let the squid rest for about 5 minutes before serving. Taste for seasoning and serve hot, accompanied if you like by hot boiled rice.

# The Cleaning and Preparation of Fresh Squid

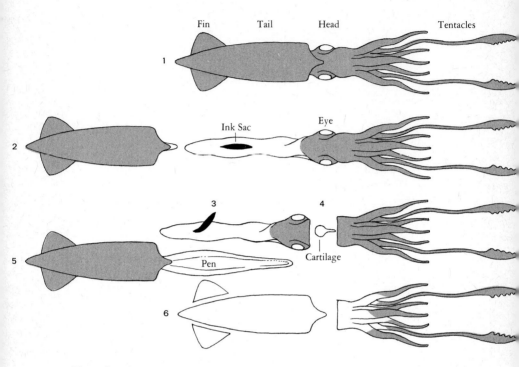

These drawings show how to take apart and
clean a fresh squid (1). First, grasp the tail
and head sections firmly in your hands and
pull the fin and outer part of the tail away
from the head and tentacles (2). Then (3)
carefully lift the silvery gray ink sac (if there
is one) from the inner section of the tail
and set it aside in a fine sieve. Next (4) use
a sharp knife to cut the tentacles free, just
beyond the eyes of the squid. Discard the
innards and eye section. With your fingers,
pop out the small round cartilage from the
core of the tentacle base. Pull the transparent
icicle-shaped pen or tail skeleton from the
inside of the tail cone (5) and discard it. Pull
the fins away from the cone-shaped tail and
set aside (6). Under cold running water,
peel the red, lacy outer membrane away from
the fins and the cone with your fingers, and
remove as much of the membrane as possible
from the tentacles. Gently invert the cone
and then wash it thoroughly.

## Calamares Rellenos en su Tinta

STUFFED SQUID IN ITS OWN INK

To serve 4

8 small fresh whole squid with ink
  sacs
½ cup olive oil
1 cup finely chopped onions
1½ teaspoons finely chopped garlic
1 tablespoon finely chopped parsley
A pinch of ground nutmeg,

preferably freshly grated
½ teaspoon salt
Freshly ground black pepper
1 cup soft fresh crumbs made from
  French or Italian bread, trimmed
  of crusts and pulverized in a
  blender or pulled apart with a fork
½ cup cold water
1 tablespoon flour

Clean the squid, following the directions in the diagrams opposite and carefully reserving the ink sacs in a small, fine sieve. Wash the tail cones, fins and tentacles under cold running water and pat them dry with paper towels. Set the tail cones aside, but chop the tentacles and fins finely.

To make the stuffing, pour ¼ cup of the olive oil into a heavy 8- to 10-inch skillet, and heat over moderate heat until a light haze forms above it. Add the chopped tentacles and fins, and, stirring constantly, cook for 1 or 2 minutes. Then stir in ½ cup of the onions, ½ teaspoon of the garlic, the parsley, nutmeg, ¼ teaspoon of the salt and a few grindings of pepper, and cook for 5 minutes, or until the onions are soft and transparent but not brown. Add the crumbs and cook, stirring frequently until all the liquid in the pan is absorbed. Set aside.

Fill each tail cone with about 2 tablespoons of the stuffing, packing it loosely to within about ½ inch of the opening. Press the open edges of the cone together and pin them securely with a toothpick.

In a heavy 10- to 12-inch skillet heat the remaining ¼ cup of olive oil over high heat until a light haze forms above it. Add the squid and the remaining ½ cup of onions, 1 teaspoon of garlic and ¼ teaspoon of salt. Distribute the onions around the squid and, stirring gently, cook over high heat for a minute or so. Then reduce the heat to the lowest possible point, cover the skillet tightly and simmer for 10 minutes.

Meanwhile, mash the ink sacs in the sieve with the back of a spoon, and press out as much ink as possible. Pour the water over the sacs and mash them again to extract any remaining ink. The ink is usually black but may be brown in color and in either case the water should become dark and opaque. Add the flour to the ink and stir vigorously with a whisk until the mixture is smooth. Then pour the mixture into the skillet of simmering squid, stir gently, cover again and simmer for 10 minutes longer.

Remove the pan from the heat and, without removing the cover, let the squid rest for about 5 minutes before serving. Taste for seasoning and serve hot, accompanied if you like by hot boiled rice.

# Meats

## Iscas

MARINATED LIVER WITH RED WINE SAUCE

To serve 4

¾ cup dry red wine
2 tablespoons red wine vinegar
1 teaspoon finely chopped garlic
½ bay leaf, crumbled
½ teaspoon salt

Freshly ground black pepper
1 pound calf's or beef liver, cut
    into ⅛-inch-thick slices
3 tablespoons olive oil
3 bacon slices, coarsely chopped
2 tablespoons finely chopped parsley

Combine the wine, vinegar, garlic, bay leaf, salt and a few grindings of pepper in a glass, enamel or stainless-steel bowl or baking dish. Add the liver, turning the slices about with a spoon until they are evenly coated. Marinate at room temperature for about 2 hours.

In a heavy 10- to 12-inch skillet, heat the olive oil over moderate heat until a light haze forms above it. Add the bacon and cook, stirring frequently, until golden brown and crisp. Drain on a double thickness of paper towels. Remove the liver slices from the marinade and pat them dry with paper towels. Reserve the marinade. Heat the bacon fat remaining in the skillet until it splutters. Add the liver and cook the slices about 2 minutes on each side, regulating the heat so they brown quickly and evenly without burning. Remove the liver to a heated platter. Quickly pour the reserved marinade into the skillet and boil it uncovered over high heat until it has reduced to about half, meanwhile scraping in any browned bits clinging to the bottom and sides of the pan. Taste for seasoning. Scatter the bacon pieces over the liver, pour the sauce over it and sprinkle with parsley. Serve at once, accompanied by Portuguese fried potatoes (*Recipe Index*).

# Bife à Portuguêsa

PORTUGUESE STEAK

To serve 4

4 large peeled garlic cloves, 2
   crushed with a cleaver or knife
   and 2 cut lengthwise into halves
1 tablespoon red wine vinegar
1 teaspoon salt
Freshly ground black pepper
4 beef tenderloin steaks, sliced about
   ¾ inch thick
2 tablespoons olive oil

2 tablespoons butter
1 large bay leaf, crumbled
8 thin slices *presunto* ham or
   prosciutto or other lean smoked
   ham
¼ cup dry red wine
1 teaspoon fresh lemon juice
2 teaspoons finely chopped parsley
1 lemon cut into 8 wedges

Preheat the oven to 250°. Mash the crushed garlic, vinegar, salt and a few grindings of pepper to a smooth paste with a mortar and pestle or in a bowl with the back of a spoon. With your fingers, rub the paste into the steaks, pressing it firmly into both sides of the meat.

In a heavy 10- to 12-inch skillet, melt the butter in the olive oil over moderate heat. When the foam has almost subsided, add the garlic halves and bay leaf and cook for 1 minute, stirring constantly. Then with a slotted spoon, remove and discard the garlic and bay leaf. Add the steaks and cook for 2 or 3 minutes on each side, turning them with tongs, and regulating the heat so that they color quickly and evenly. The steaks should be well browned, but still pink inside.

Transfer the steaks to individual baking dishes or fairly deep plates and keep them warm in the oven. Add the slices of ham to the fat remaining in the skillet and cook over high heat, turning them frequently for 1 or 2 minutes. With the tongs, place 2 slices of ham on each steak. Pour off all but a thin film of fat from the skillet, add the wine and lemon juice and bring to a boil over high heat, meanwhile scraping in any brown particles clinging to the bottom and sides of the pan. Pour the sauce over the steaks, sprinkle them with parsley and garnish each serving with lemon wedges. Serve at once. *Bife à portuguêsa* is usually served with fried potato slices (*Recipe Index*) carefully arranged around the edges of the serving dishes.

## Ternera a la Sevillana
SAUTÉED VEAL WITH SHERRY AND GREEN OLIVES

To serve 6

12 pitted green Spanish olives
1 cup olive oil
2 cups finely chopped onions
1 tablespoon finely chopped garlic
2 small green peppers, deribbed,
  seeded and finely chopped
¼ pound fresh mushrooms, sliced
  ⅛ inch thick (about 2 cups sliced)
4 medium-sized tomatoes peeled,
  seeded, and finely chopped (see
  huevos a la flamenca, page 68)
½ cup finely diced serrano ham, or

substitute ⅛ pound prosciutto or
  other lean smoked ham
2 tablespoons blanched almonds,
  pulverized in a blender or with a
  nut grinder or mortar and pestle
Salt
Freshly ground black pepper
1 cup flour
6 veal scallops, cut about ⅜ inch
  thick and pounded ¼ inch thick
½ cup pale dry sherry
½ cup water

In a small glass, enameled, or stainless-steel saucepan, bring 2 cups of water to a boil over high heat. Drop in the olives, reduce the heat to low and simmer for 2 minutes. Drain the olives in a sieve or colander and run cold water over them to stop their cooking. Set aside.

For the *sofrito,* heat ½ cup of the olive oil in a heavy 10- to 12-inch skillet over moderate heat until a light haze forms above it. Add the onions, garlic and green pepper and stirring frequently, cook for 5 minutes, or until the vegetables are soft but not brown. Add the mushrooms, tomatoes, olives, ham and pulverized almonds, and bring to a boil, stirring constantly. Cook briskly until most of the liquid in the pan evaporates and the mixture is thick enough to hold its shape lightly in a spoon. Set aside.

Sprinkle the veal scallops liberally with salt and a few grindings of pepper. Dip them in the flour and shake them vigorously to remove all but a light dusting. Heat the remaining ½ cup of oil in another 10- to 12-inch skillet until a light haze forms above it. Cook the scallops (in two batches if necessary) for 3 or 4 minutes on each side, turning them with tongs and regulating the heat so that they brown quickly and evenly without burning.

As they brown, transfer the scallops to a plate. Discard the oil remaining in the pan and in its place pour in the sherry and water. Bring to a boil over high heat, meanwhile scraping in any brown particles clinging to the bottom and sides of the skillet. Then add the reserved *sofrito* and stir together thoroughly. Taste the sauce for seasoning.

Return the veal to the skillet, lower the heat, cover tightly and simmer for 4 or 5 minutes, or until the scallops are tender when pierced with the point of a small, sharp knife.

To serve, arrange the scallops attractively in a row down the center of a deep heated platter, overlapping them slightly, pour the sauce evenly over them and serve at once.


## Trouxa de Vitela
MARINATED VEAL ROAST WITH RED ONION

To serve 6 to 8

| | |
|---|---|
| 1 cup olive oil | pepper |
| ⅓ cup white wine vinegar | 2 teaspoons salt |
| 1 large red onion, peeled and finely chopped | ½ teaspoon freshly ground black pepper |
| ½ teaspoon finely chopped garlic | A 3½- to 4-pound boneless veal roast, preferably cut from the leg or rump and securely tied |
| 2 tablespoons finely chopped parsley | |
| ¼ teaspoon crushed dried hot red | |

For the marinade, combine ¾ cup of the oil, the vinegar, onion, garlic, parsley, red pepper, salt and black pepper in a small bowl and stir well. Place the veal in a deep bowl just large enough to hold it comfortably, and pour in the marinade, turning the veal about with a large spoon until it is moistened on all sides. Marinate at room temperature for 4 hours or in the refrigerator for at least 8 hours, turning it over two or three times as it marinates.

Preheat the oven to 450°. Remove the veal from the marinade, brush off any bits of onion or spice clinging to it, and place it on a rack in a shallow roasting pan. Set the marinade aside in a small saucepan. Roast the veal in the middle of the oven for 20 minutes. Then baste it with a tablespoon or so of olive oil and reduce the heat to 350°. Basting two or three more times with the remaining olive oil, continue to roast for about 1½ hours longer, or until the veal is tender.

Then bring the reserved marinade to a boil over high heat, reduce the heat to low and simmer for 5 minutes. To serve, carve the veal into ¼-inch slices, arrange them attractively on a large heated platter and pour the simmering marinade over them. Serve at once.

## Riñones al Jerez

SAUTÉED KIDNEYS WITH SHERRY SAUCE

To serve 6

6 tablespoons olive oil
1 cup finely chopped onions
1 teaspoon finely chopped garlic
1 small bay leaf
2 tablespoons flour
½ cup beef or chicken stock, fresh
    or canned

2 tablespoons finely chopped parsley
2 pounds veal kidneys, split
    lengthwise in half, trimmed of all
    fat, and cut into 1-inch cubes
Salt
Freshly ground black pepper
½ cup pale dry sherry

In a heavy 8- to 10-inch skillet, heat 4 tablespoons of the olive oil over moderate heat until a light haze forms above it. Add the onions, garlic and bay leaf. Stirring frequently, cook for 5 minutes, or until the onions are soft and transparent but not brown. Add the flour and mix thoroughly. Pour in the stock and, stirring constantly, cook over high heat until the mixture thickens heavily and comes to a boil. Add the parsley, reduce the heat to low, and simmer for about 3 minutes. Set aside.

Heat the remaining 2 tablespoons of olive oil in a heavy 10- to 12-inch skillet. Sprinkle the kidneys liberally with salt and a few grindings of pepper. Then cook them in the hot oil for 4 or 5 minutes, turning them about with a large spoon and regulating the heat so that they brown quickly on all sides without burning.

Transfer the kidneys to a plate and pour the sherry into the pan. Bring to a boil over high heat, meanwhile scraping in any brown particles clinging to the bottom and sides of the pan. Return the kidneys to the pan, stir in the reserved onion sauce and bring to a boil. Reduce the heat to low, simmer a minute or two and taste for seasoning.

Serve the kidneys at once, accompanied if you like by saffron rice *(Recipe Index)* and garnished with strips of pimiento.

## *Lombo de Porco com Pimentos Vermelhos Doces*

MARINATED PORK LOIN WITH SWEET RED PEPPERS

To serve 4 to 6

1 tablespoon finely chopped garlic
1 teaspoon salt, preferably coarse
   salt
½ teaspoon freshly ground black
   pepper
2 pounds boneless pork loin, cut
   into ¼-inch-thick slices
¼ cup lard
4 medium-sized sweet red peppers,

seeded, deribbed and cut
   lengthwise into ½-inch-wide
   strips, or substitute 1½ cups
   drained, canned pimientos, cut
   lengthwise into ½-inch strips
1 cup dry white wine
½ cup chicken stock, fresh or canned
1 lemon, cut lengthwise into 8
   wedges

With a mortar and pestle or the back of a large heavy spoon, mash the garlic, salt and pepper together to a smooth paste. Lightly spread the pork slices with the paste, place them in a bowl and toss with a spoon. Cover tightly and marinate at room temperature for 2 or 3 hours, or in the refrigerator for 6 hours, turning the pork about in the bowl from time to time.

In a heavy 10- to 12-inch skillet, melt the lard over high heat. Brown the pork in the hot fat (in two or three batches if necessary), turning the slices with tongs and regulating the heat so that the slices color quickly and evenly on both sides without burning. As they brown, transfer them to a plate.

Add the red peppers to the fat remaining in the pan and, stirring frequently, cook them for about 5 minutes, or until they are well coated with the fat but not brown. (The canned pimiento strips need only be cooked until they are coated with fat.) Transfer the peppers to the plate with the meat. Pour off all but a thin film of fat from the skillet and add the wine and stock. Bring to a boil over high heat, meanwhile scraping into the liquid any brown particles clinging to the bottom and sides of the pan.

Return the pork and peppers to the skillet, cover tightly, and reduce the heat to low. Simmer for about 25 minutes, or until the pork is tender and shows no resistance when pierced with the point of a small, sharp knife.

With a slotted spoon, transfer the pork and peppers to a deep, heated platter. Bring the liquid remaining in the skillet to a boil over high heat, stirring constantly and cook briskly until it thickens lightly. Taste for seasoning, then pour the sauce over the meat. Serve garnished with lemon wedges.

## Carne de Porco com Amêijoas à Alentejana
### MARINATED PORK WITH CLAMS, TOMATOES AND CORIANDER

To serve 4

1½ cups dry white wine
1 tablespoon paprika
2½ teaspoons salt
Freshly ground black pepper
2 garlic cloves, cut in half
1 small bay leaf
2 pounds lean boneless pork, cut
    into 1-inch cubes
3 tablespoons lard
2 medium-sized onions, thinly sliced
1 large sweet red pepper, seeded,
    deribbed and cut lengthwise into

½-inch strips, or ⅓ cup canned
    pimientos, cut into ½-inch strips
2 teaspoons finely chopped garlic
2 medium-sized tomatoes, peeled,
    seeded and finely chopped (see
    *huevos a la flamenca, page 68*)
⅛ teaspoon crushed dried hot red
    pepper
2 dozen small hard-shelled clams,
    washed and thoroughly scrubbed
¼ cup finely chopped fresh coriander
    (*cilantro*)
1 lemon, cut into 6 or 8 wedges

In a large bowl, combine the wine, paprika, 1½ teaspoons of the salt and ¼ teaspoon black pepper and stir until thoroughly blended. Add the halved garlic cloves and bay leaf and then the cubed pork, turning the meat about in the marinade to coat the pieces evenly. Marinate for 3 hours at room temperature or in the refrigerator for 6 hours, turning the meat occasionally to keep it well moistened.

Drain the pork through a fine sieve set over a bowl and pat the cubes completely dry with paper towels. Discard the garlic and bay leaf, but reserve the marinade. In a heavy 10- to 12-inch skillet, melt 1 tablespoon of lard over high heat until it splutters. Add the pork and turn the cubes frequently, regulating the heat so that the meat colors quickly and evenly without burning. With a slotted spoon, transfer the pork to a bowl. Pour the reserved marinade into the skillet and bring to a boil over high heat, meanwhile scraping in any brown particles clinging to the bottom and sides of the pan. Boil briskly, uncovered, until the marinade is reduced to 1 cup, then pour it over the pork and set aside.

In a heavy 6- to 8-quart casserole, melt the remaining 2 tablespoons of lard over moderate heat until it splutters. Add the onion and red pepper or pimiento and, stirring frequently, cook for 5 minutes or until the vegetables are soft but not brown. Add the chopped garlic and the tomatoes, crushed hot red pepper, the remaining 1 teaspoon of salt and a few grindings of pepper. Simmer, stirring constantly for 3 or 4 minutes. Spread the clams hinged side down over the tomato sauce, cover the casserole tightly, and cook over high heat for 10 minutes, or until the clams open. (Discard those that remain closed.) Stir in the reserved pork and all its juices and simmer for 5 minutes to heat the meat through. Then sprinkle the top with coriander and garnish with the lemon wedges. Serve at once, directly from the casserole.

## Carne de Vinho e Alhos
PORK BRAISED IN WHITE WINE WITH HERBS

To serve 4

| | |
|---|---|
| 1 cup dry white wine | pepper |
| ¼ cup white wine vinegar | 2 pounds lean boneless pork, sliced |
| 1½ teaspoons finely chopped garlic | ½ inch thick and cut into strips |
| 1 medium-sized bay leaf, crumbled | 1½ inches long and ½ inch wide |
| 4 whole cloves | 5 tablespoons lard |
| 1 teaspoon savory, crumbled | 3 slices white bread, preferably |
| 1 teaspoon marjoram, crumbled | homemade type, trimmed of crusts |
| 1 teaspoon salt | and cut diagonally into 4 triangles |
| ½ teaspoon freshly ground black | 1 orange, cut into 8 wedges |

In a large bowl, combine the wine, vinegar, garlic, bay leaf, cloves, savory, marjoram, salt and pepper. Drop in the pork strips and turn them about until they are well moistened. Marinate for at least 4 hours at room temperature or 8 hours in the refrigerator, turning the meat over from time to time.

Remove the pork from the marinade and pat it completely dry with paper towels. Reserve the marinade. In a heavy 10- to 12-inch skillet, melt 1 tablespoon of the lard over moderate heat until it splutters. Add the pork and brown it well, turning the strips with tongs and regulating the heat so they color quickly and evenly without burning. Pour off all but a thin film of fat from the skillet and add ½ cup of the marinade. Bring to a boil over high heat, meanwhile scraping in any brown particles clinging to the bottom and sides of the pan. Reduce the heat to low, cover tightly and simmer for 30 minutes, or until the meat is tender and shows no resistance when pierced with the point of a small, sharp knife.

Meanwhile, in another 10- to 12-inch skillet, heat the remaining 4 tablespoons of lard over moderate heat until it splutters. Add the bread triangles and brown them well on both sides. Then drain on paper towels.

To serve, discard the cloves and then transfer the pork and its sauce to a heated platter. Garnish the platter with the bread and the orange wedges.

## Rojões Comino
BRAISED PORK WITH CUMIN, CORIANDER AND LEMON

To serve 4

2 pounds lean boneless pork, cut
    into 1-inch cubes
1 tablespoon lard
¾ cup dry white wine
1½ teaspoons ground cumin seed

½ teaspoon finely chopped garlic
1 teaspoon salt
Freshly ground black pepper
5 thin lemon slices, quartered
2 tablespoons finely chopped fresh
    coriander (*cilantro*)

Pat the pork cubes thoroughly dry with paper towels. In a heavy 10- to 12-inch skillet, melt the lard over high heat until it splutters. Add the pork cubes and brown them, turning the cubes frequently with a large spoon and regulating the heat so that they color quickly and evenly without burning. Stir in ½ cup of wine, the cumin, garlic, salt and a liberal grinding of pepper. Bring to a boil, then cover the skillet, reduce the heat to low and simmer for 25 minutes, or until the pork is tender and shows no resistance when pierced with the tip of a small, sharp knife. Add the remaining ¼ cup of wine and the lemon slices and cook over high heat, turning the meat and lemon pieces constantly, until the sauce thickens ever so slightly. Stir in the coriander and taste for seasoning.

    Pour the pork mixture onto the center of a large heated platter and surround it if you like with Portuguese fried potatoes (*Recipe Index*).


## Lomo de Cerdo a la Zaragozana
PORK CHOPS WITH TOMATO SAUCE AND BLACK OLIVES

To serve 6

6 lean loin pork chops, cut about 1
    inch thick (about 3 pounds)
Salt
Freshly ground black pepper
½ cup flour
¼ cup olive oil
1 cup finely chopped onions
½ teaspoon finely chopped garlic
1 small bay leaf
3 medium-sized tomatoes peeled,
    seeded and finely chopped (*see*

*huevos a la flamenca, page 68*), or
    substitute 1 cup chopped, drained,
    canned tomatoes
½ cup finely chopped *serrano* ham,
    or substitute ⅛ pound prosciutto
    or other lean smoked ham
½ cup dry white wine
1 cup water
1 hard-cooked egg, finely chopped
2 tablespoons finely chopped parsley
12 pitted Spanish black olives, cut
    lengthwise into halves

Sprinkle the pork chops liberally with salt and a few grindings of pepper. Dip them in flour and shake each one vigorously to remove the excess. In a heavy 10- to 12-inch skillet, heat the oil over high heat until a light haze forms above it. Add the chops (in 2 batches if necessary) and brown them well, turning them with tongs and regulating the heat so that they color quickly and evenly without burning.

Transfer the chops to a plate and add the onions, garlic and bay leaf to the fat remaining in the skillet. Cook over moderate heat for 5 minutes, or until the onions are soft and transparent but not brown. Add the tomatoes and ham, raise the heat and cook briskly, stirring frequently until most of the liquid in the pan evaporates and the mixture is thick enough to hold its shape lightly in a spoon.

Stir in the wine, water, egg, parsley and olives, and bring to a boil again. Return the chops to the skillet, and baste them thoroughly with the sauce. Cover tightly, reduce the heat to its lowest point, and simmer for about 30 to 40 minutes, or until the chops are tender. To serve, arrange the chops attractively on a heated platter and pour the sauce over them.


## Cochifrito

FRICASSEE OF LAMB WITH LEMON AND GARLIC

To serve 4

| | |
|---|---|
| 2 pounds lean boneless shoulder of lamb, cut into 1-inch cubes | ½ teaspoon finely chopped garlic |
| Salt | 1 tablespoon paprika |
| Freshly ground black pepper | 2 tablespoons finely chopped parsley |
| ¼ cup olive oil | 2 tablespoons fresh lemon juice |
| 1 cup finely chopped onions | 1 lemon cut lengthwise into 8 wedges (optional) |

Sprinkle the lamb liberally with salt and a few grindings of pepper. In a heavy 10- to 12-inch skillet, heat the olive oil over high heat until a light haze forms above it. Add the lamb and brown it well, turning the pieces with tongs and regulating the heat so that the meat colors evenly without burning. With a slotted spoon, transfer the lamb to a plate.

Add the onions and garlic to the fat remaining in the skillet and, stirring frequently, cook for about 5 minutes, or until the onions are soft and transparent but not brown. Stir in the paprika, then return the lamb and any juices that have collected around it to the skillet. Add the parsley and lemon juice and reduce the heat to low. Cover tightly and simmer for about 1 hour, or until the lamb is tender and shows no resistance when pierced with the point of a small, sharp knife. Taste for seasoning and serve at once from a heated platter, garnished if you like with lemon wedges.

## Chuletas de Cordero a la Navarra

LAMB CHOPS AND SAUSAGES IN TOMATO SAUCE

To serve 4

1/4 cup olive oil
8 lean lamb chops, cut 1/2 inch thick
Salt

Freshly ground black pepper
2 *chorizos,* or substitute 1/3 pound
    other garlic-seasoned smoked pork
    sausage

Preheat the oven to 375°. In a heavy 10- to 12-inch skillet, heat the oil over high heat until a light haze forms above it. Sprinkle the chops liberally with salt and a few grindings of pepper. Then brown them in the oil, turning them with tongs and regulating the heat so that they color quickly and evenly without burning. Arrange the chops in a baking dish just large enough to hold them comfortably in one layer and set aside.

Place the sausages in a 6- to 8-inch skillet and prick them in two or three places with the point of a small, sharp knife. Add enough cold water to cover them completely and bring to a boil over high heat. Then reduce the heat to low and simmer uncovered for 5 minutes. Drain on paper towels, then slice the sausages into 1/4-inch-thick rounds  Set aside.

SOFRITO

1 cup finely chopped onions
1 teaspoon finely chopped garlic
1/2 cup finely diced *serrano* ham, or
    substitute 1/8 pound prosciutto or
    other lean smoked ham
4 medium-sized tomatoes peeled,
    seeded and finely chopped *(see*

*huevos a la flamenca, page 68 ),* or
    substitute 1 1/2 cups finely chopped,
    drained, canned tomatoes
1 small bay leaf, crumbled
1/4 teaspoon thyme, crumbled
1/2 cup water
1 tablespoon finely chopped parsley

To make the *sofrito,* add the onions and garlic to the fat remaining in the skillet and, stirring frequently, cook for 5 minutes, or until the onions are soft and transparent but not brown. Add the ham and cook for a minute or two, then add the tomatoes, bay leaf, thyme and water. Bring to a boil and cook briskly for about 5 minutes, or until most of the liquid in the pan evaporates and the mixture holds its shape lightly in a spoon. Taste for seasoning.

Scatter the sausage slices over the chops and spread the *sofrito* evenly over them. Bake uncovered in the middle of the oven for about 20 minutes, or until the chops are tender. Sprinkle them with the parsley and serve at once, directly from the baking dish.

## Cordeiro à Transmontana
ROLLED LEG OF LAMB ROASTED WITH MINT

To serve 6 to 8

| | |
|---|---|
| ¼ cup finely chopped parsley | 1 teaspoon paprika |
| ¼ cup finely cut fresh mint leaves | 1 teaspoon salt |
| 2 tablespoons butter, softened | ¼ teaspoon freshly ground black |
| 2 tablespoons finely chopped lean | pepper |
| bacon | A 6 to 7 pound leg of lamb, boned, |
| 2 teaspoons finely chopped garlic | with outer fell and all fat removed |
| 1 tablespoon red wine vinegar | 2 tablespoons olive oil |

In a large bowl, combine the parsley, mint, butter, bacon, garlic, vinegar, paprika, salt and black pepper, and mix them together thoroughly.

With a large, sharp knife, open the leg of lamb flat by cutting lengthwise through the thinnest side of the cavity left when the bones were removed. Cut away any clumps of exposed fat from inside the leg and, with the point of the knife, cut ¼ to ½ inch down into the thicker areas so that the lamb lies even flatter. Spread the leg out flat, fat side down, and pat the parsley and mint mixture evenly over the meat. Then, starting at one long side, roll the lamb into a tight cylinder, tucking in the ragged edges of meat. With white kitchen cord, tie the roll securely at two-inch intervals, wrap it loosely in foil or plastic wrap, and refrigerate for at least 12 hours.

Preheat the oven to 450°. With a pastry brush, coat the surface of the lamb with the olive oil. Place the meat on a rack in a shallow roasting pan just large enough to hold it comfortably. For the most predictable results, insert a meat thermometer into the center of the meat. Roast uncovered in the middle of the oven for 15 minutes. Then reduce the heat to 350° and continue roasting uncovered 45 minutes to 1 hour, or until the lamb is done to your taste. Basting is unnecessary. The meat thermometer will register 130° to 140° when the lamb is rare, 150° to 160° when medium and 160° to 170° when it is well done.

Carve the lamb crosswise into ¼-inch-thick slices and arrange them slightly overlapping along the center of a heated platter. Serve at once.

In Portugal, this roast is prepared with a leg of kid *(cabrito)* rather than lamb—and you may substitute kid if it is available in your locality.

## Arroz con Costra

RABBIT AND RICE CASSEROLE WITH EGG CRUST

To serve 4

| | |
|---|---|
| ½ cup dried chick-peas (garbanzos) | 1 teaspoon finely chopped garlic |
| 2 quarts water | 1 small bay leaf |
| A 2- to 2½-pound rabbit, thoroughly defrosted if frozen, cut into 8 serving pieces | 3 *chorizos*, or substitute ½ pound other garlic-seasoned smoked pork sausage |
| Salt | 1 cup raw medium or long-grain regular-milled rice or imported short-grain rice |
| Freshly ground black pepper | |
| ¼ cup olive oil | |
| 1 cup finely chopped onions | 4 eggs, lightly beaten |

Starting a day ahead, wash the chick-peas in a sieve under cold running water. Then place them in a bowl or pan and add enough water to cover them by 2 inches. Soak at room temperature for at least 12 hours.

Drain the chick-peas in a sieve or colander and place them in a heavy 3- to 4-quart casserole. Add 2 quarts of fresh water. Bring to a boil over high heat, reduce the heat to low, and simmer partially covered for 1 hour.

Meanwhile, pat the rabbit thoroughly dry with paper towels and sprinkle the pieces liberally with salt and a few grindings of pepper. In a heavy 10- to 12-inch skillet, heat the olive oil over high heat until a light haze forms above it. Add the rabbit and brown it well, turning the pieces with tongs and regulating the heat so that they color evenly without burning. As the pieces are browned, transfer them to a plate.

When the chick-peas have simmered for their allotted hour, add the rabbit, onions, garlic, bay leaf and ½ teaspoon of salt and stir the mixture gently. Then cover tightly and simmer for 1 more hour.

Meanwhile, place the sausages in an 8- to 10-inch skillet and prick them in two or three places with the point of a small, sharp knife. Add enough cold water to cover them completely and bring to a boil over high heat. Reduce the heat to low and simmer uncovered for 5 minutes. Drain on paper towels, then slice the sausages into ¼-inch-thick rounds.

At the end of the second hour stir the sausages and rice into the casserole, cover and simmer for 30 minutes longer, or until the rice, chick-peas and rabbit are tender and most of the liquid in the casserole has been absorbed by the rice. Taste for seasoning.

Preheat the oven to 350°. Pour the beaten eggs over the ingredients in the casserole (do not stir) and bake uncovered in the middle of the oven for 10 minutes, or until the eggs are firm and lightly browned. Serve at once, directly from the casserole.

# Conejo a la Ampurdanesa

RABBIT BRAISED IN WINE WITH CHOCOLATE

To serve 4

4 tablespoons lard
¼ pound salt pork, finely diced
A 2½- to 3-pound rabbit, thoroughly
    defrosted if frozen, cut into 8
    serving pieces
Salt
Freshly ground black pepper
12 whole peeled white onions, each
    about 1 inch in diameter
1 tablespoon flour
½ cup dry red wine

2 cups water
1 small bay leaf, crumbled
2 tablespoons finely chopped parsley
¼ teaspoon thyme, crumbled
¼ cup blanched almonds combined
    with ¼ cup pine nuts *(pignoli)*
    and pulverized in a blender or
    with a nut grinder or mortar and
    pestle
2 teaspoons finely grated
    unsweetened baking chocolate

In a heavy 4- to 5-quart casserole, melt the lard and add the pork dice. Stirring frequently, cook over moderate heat until the pork dice have rendered all their fat and are brown and crisp. With a slotted spoon, transfer the pork to paper towels to drain.

Pat the pieces of rabbit completely dry with paper towels. Season them liberally with salt and a few grindings of pepper. Add the rabbit to the fat remaining in the casserole and brown it well, turning the pieces with tongs and regulating the heat so that they color quickly and evenly without burning. Avoid crowding the pan; if necessary brown the rabbit in two batches. As the pieces brown, transfer them to a plate.

Add the onions to the casserole and brown them, shaking the casserole occasionally to roll them around and color them as evenly as possible. With a slotted spoon, transfer them to the plate with the rabbit. Pour off all but a thin film of fat from the casserole and stir in the flour. Cook for a minute or so until the flour browns lightly. Then pour in the wine and water and bring to a boil over high heat, meanwhile scraping in any brown particles clinging to the bottom and sides of the casserole. Add the bay leaf, parsley, thyme, and the reserved pork dice and rabbit, reduce the heat to low and cover tightly. Simmer undisturbed for 30 minutes.

Meanwhile, with a mortar and pestle or with the back of a large spoon, mash the almonds, pine nuts and chocolate together. Add them to the casserole with the reserved onions, stir thoroughly, and cover again. Simmer for 30 minutes longer, or until the rabbit is tender and the meat shows no resistance when pierced with the point of a small, sharp knife. Taste for seasoning. Serve at once, directly from the casserole.

# Tripas à Moda do Porto

TRIPE STEW WITH VEAL, CHICKEN, SAUSAGE, HAM AND BEANS

To serve 6

1½ pounds tripe, cut into 1½-inch
   squares
A meaty veal shank (about 1 pound)
2 teaspoons salt
1 cup dried white navy or pea beans
½ pound *linguiça*, or substitute
   *chorizo* or other garlic-seasoned
   smoked pork sausage
¼ pound *presunto* ham, or substitute
   *serrano*, prosciutto or other lean
   smoked ham
A 1½- to 2-pound chicken, cut into

6 or 8 pieces
2 large carrots, scraped and sliced
   into ¼-inch-thick rounds
1 large onion, peeled and cut
   crosswise into ⅛-inch-thick slices
3 tablespoons lard
1 cup coarsely chopped onions
2 tablespoons ground cumin
1 teaspoon freshly ground black
   pepper
1 small bay leaf
¼ cup finely chopped parsley
6 cups hot boiled rice (2 cups raw rice)

Combine the tripe, veal shank and salt in a heavy 4- to 5-quart saucepan and pour in enough cold water to cover the meat by at least 2 inches. Bring to a boil over high heat, skimming off the scum and foam as they rise to the surface. Partially cover the pan, reduce the heat to its lowest point and simmer for 2 hours, or until the tripe is tender.

Meanwhile, combine the beans and 2 quarts of water in a heavy 3- to 4-quart saucepan. Bring to a boil over high heat and boil briskly for 2 minutes. Remove the pan from the heat and let the beans soak for 1 hour. Then bring them to a boil in the soaking water, lower the heat and simmer partially covered for 1 to 1½ hours, or until the beans are tender but still intact. Drain the beans thoroughly and set aside.

While the beans are cooking, place the sausages in an 8- to 10-inch skillet and prick them in two or three places with the point of a small, sharp knife. Add enough cold water to cover them completely, and bring to a boil over high heat. Then reduce the heat to low, and simmer uncovered for 5 minutes. Drain on paper towels.

Combine the sausages, ham and chicken in another heavy 3- to 4-quart saucepan. Pour in enough cold water to cover the meat and chicken by at least 1 inch, and bring to a boil over high heat. Skim the surface of all foam and scum, reduce the heat to low, and simmer partially covered for 15 minutes. Add the carrots and sliced onions, and simmer for 15 minutes longer, or until the meats and vegetables are tender. Drain in a large sieve set over a bowl. Let the broth rest a few minutes, then skim the surface of all fat. With a small, sharp knife, remove the skin from the chicken and cut the flesh away from the bones. Discard the skin and bones. Cut the chicken into 2-by-¼-inch strips, slice the sausages crosswise into ⅛-inch-thick slices and cut the ham into ½-inch cubes. Set the cut meats and the vegetables and broth aside.

Drain the tripe and veal shank, discarding their cooking liquid. Set the tripe aside on a plate and, with a small knife, cut the veal away from the shank. Discard the bone and cut the veal into small pieces.

In a heavy 5- to 6-quart casserole, melt the lard over moderate heat until it splutters. Add the chopped onions, cumin and pepper and, stirring frequently, cook for 5 minutes, or until the onions are soft and transparent but not brown. Add the tripe, veal, chicken, sausage, ham, carrots, sliced onion, beans, bay leaf and parsley. Pour in 3 cups of the reserved broth and bring to a boil over moderate heat. Reduce the heat to its lowest point, cover the casserole, and simmer for 10 minutes. Taste for seasoning: The stew should have a distinct flavor of cumin and pepper, so if necessary add more. Serve directly from the casserole, accompanied by a large bowl of hot boiled rice.

## Callos a la Madrileña
TRIPE STEW WITH CALF'S FEET, HAM AND SAUSAGES

To serve 8 to 10

| | |
|---|---|
| 2 pounds calf's feet (about 3 feet), sawed, not chopped, into 3-inch pieces, or substitute 2 pounds fresh pig's feet sawed into 3-inch pieces | 1 small head of garlic, trimmed of root fibers and dry outer casing, but not peeled or separated into individual cloves |
| 4 chorizos, or substitute ¾ pound other garlic-seasoned smoked pork sausage | 2 small bay leaves |
| | 3 parsley sprigs |
| | 2 teaspoons salt |
| 3 pounds tripe, cut into 2-inch squares | 4 quarts water |
| 2 cups coarsely chopped onions | ½ pound serrano ham, cut into ½-inch cubes, or substitute prosciutto or other smoked ham |

Blanch the calf's feet in a large saucepan by covering them with cold water, bringing the water to a boil over high heat and cooking them briskly for 2 minutes. Drain and rinse thoroughly under cold running water.

Place the sausages in an 8- to 10-inch skillet and prick them in two or three places with the tip of a small, sharp knife. Add enough cold water to cover them completely and bring to a boil over high heat. Then reduce the heat to low and simmer uncovered for 5 minutes. Drain on paper towels.

In a heavy 8- to 10-quart casserole, combine the calf's feet, tripe, onions, head of garlic, bay leaves, parsley, salt and water. Bring to a boil over high heat, reduce the heat to low, partially cover the casserole and simmer for 2 hours. Then add the ham, partially cover again, and cook for 1 hour longer.

*Continued on next page*

SOFRITO

2 tablespoons olive oil
½ cup finely chopped onions
1 tablespoon finely chopped garlic
3 medium-sized tomatoes, peeled,
  seeded and finely chopped (*see*

*huevos a la flamenca, page 68*), or
  substitute 1 cup chopped,
  drained, canned tomatoes
1 teaspoon paprika
½ teaspoon cayenne pepper

Meanwhile, prepare the *sofrito*. In a heavy 8- to 10-inch skillet, heat the olive oil over moderate heat until a light haze forms above it. Add the onions and garlic and, stirring frequently, cook for 5 minutes, or until the onions are soft and transparent but not brown. Stir in the tomatoes, paprika, and cayenne pepper, bring to a boil and cook briskly, uncovered, until most of the liquid in the pan evaporates and the mixture is thick enough to hold its shape lightly in a spoon.

Ladle about 1 cup of the tripe stock into the *sofrito* and stir until well blended. Then pour the mixture slowly into the simmering casserole, stirring constantly. Add the *chorizos*, and simmer partially covered for 30 minutes.

To serve, remove and discard the head of garlic. Transfer the calf's feet and sausages to a plate. With a small, sharp knife cut the calf's feet meat away from the bones. Remove the fat and gristle and cut the meat into small pieces. Slice the sausages into ½-inch-thick rounds, then return the meats to the casserole. Taste for seasoning, and ladle the stew into a heated tureen. Because of the large amount of natural gelatin in the tripe and calf's feet, it is important that the stew be served very hot and in heated soup plates. If the plates are cold, the gelatin will thicken to a gummy consistency.

## Cozido à Portuguêsa
BOILED MEATS, CHICKEN AND VEGETABLES

To serve 8

1 cup dried chick-peas (garbanzos)
3 pounds beef rump or round
A 1-pound smoked ham hock
Salt
4 quarts water
1 large onion, peeled and quartered
½ pound *linguiça* or substitute ½
   pound *chorizo* or other garlic-
   seasoned smoked pork sausage
A 1½-to 2-pound chicken, cut into
   6 to 8 serving pieces
4 medium-sized sweet potatoes,
   peeled and halved
4 medium-sized boiling potatoes,
   peeled and halved
3 medium-sized white turnips, peeled
   and cut lengthwise into quarters
4 medium-sized carrots, scraped and
   cut lengthwise into halves
1 medium-sized white cabbage, cut
   in half lengthwise, cored and
   sliced into 8 wedges
4 cups coarsely chopped turnip
   greens
1 cup raw medium or long-grain
   regular-milled rice or imported
   short-grain rice
Freshly ground black pepper
2 tablespoons finely chopped parsley

Starting a day ahead, wash the chick-peas in a sieve under cold running water, then place them in a pan or bowl and add enough cold water to cover them by 2 inches. Soak at room temperature for at least 12 hours.

In a heavy 8- to 10-quart casserole, combine the beef, ham hock and 1 teaspoon of salt. Pour in enough water to cover the meat by 2 inches, and bring to a boil over high heat, meanwhile skimming off the foam and scum as they rise to the surface. Reduce the heat to low, add the onion, partially cover the pan, and simmer for 2 hours. Drain the chick-peas and add them. Simmer partially covered for 1 hour longer. The meats should always be covered with the liquid. Replenish it when necessary with boiling water.

Meanwhile, place the sausages in a small skillet and prick them in two or three places with the point of a knife. Add enough cold water to cover them completely and bring to a boil over high heat. Then reduce the heat to low and simmer uncovered for 5 minutes. Drain on paper towels.

With a ladle, transfer 2 cups of the meat and chick-pea broth to a heavy 1- to 1½-quart saucepan and set it aside. Add the sausages, chicken, sweet potatoes, white potatoes, turnips and carrots to the casserole, cover and simmer for 40 minutes. Add the cabbage and turnip greens and cook 20 to 30 minutes longer, or until the meat and all the vegetables are tender.

Meanwhile bring the reserved 2 cups of broth to a boil over high heat. Stirring constantly, pour in the rice, add 1 teaspoon of salt and reduce the heat to low. Cover tightly and cook for 20 minutes, or until the rice has absorbed all the broth. Add more salt and pepper to taste.

To serve, transfer the chicken and meat to a carving board. With a small, sharp knife, remove the skin and bones of the chicken and trim any pieces of meat from the ham hock. Cut the beef and sausages into ¼-inch-thick slices. Arrange the meats and vegetables on a heated platter and moisten them with a few spoonfuls of the cooking liquid. Sprinkle with parsley and serve accompanied by the rice. (Serve the cooking broth as a first course or re-serve it for use in such soups as *sopa da panela, Recipe Index.*)

## Cocido Madrileño

BOILED CHICKEN, MEATS AND VEGETABLES

To serve 6 to 8

1 cup (½ pound) dried chick-peas (garbanzos)
5½ quarts water
A 5- to 6-pound stewing fowl
2 pounds lean fresh beef brisket
1 pound boneless *serrano* ham, or substitute prosciutto or other lean smoked ham
½ pound salt pork, rind removed
1 large onion, peeled
2 medium-sized carrots, scraped
2 medium-sized leeks, including 2

inches of the green stems
1 tablespoon finely chopped garlic
1 small bay leaf
4 parsley sprigs
½ teaspoon freshly ground black pepper
6 *chorizos,* or substitute 1 pound other garlic-seasoned smoked pork sausages
A 2-pound white cabbage, trimmed, cut lengthwise into 6 wedges and cored
6 small potatoes, peeled

Starting a day ahead, wash the chick-peas thoroughly in a sieve or colander under cold running water, then combine them with 2 quarts of cold water in a heavy 10- to 12-quart casserole. The water should cover them by about an inch; add more water if necessary. Soak the chick-peas at room temperature for at least 12 hours.

Drain the peas in a sieve or colander and return them to the casserole. Add 5½ quarts of fresh cold water, the stewing fowl and beef brisket to the casserole, and bring to a boil over high heat, meanwhile skimming off the foam and scum as they rise to the surface. Reduce the heat to low and sim-mer partially covered for 1½ hours. Then add the ham, salt pork, onion, car-rots, leeks, garlic, bay leaf, parsley and black pepper, and cook partially covered for 30 minutes longer.

Meanwhile, place the sausages in a 10- to 12-inch skillet and prick them in two or three places with the point of a small, sharp knife. Add enough water to cover them completely and bring to a boil over moderate heat. Re-duce the heat to low and simmer uncovered for 5 minutes, then discard the cooking liquid and transfer the sausages to the casserole. Add the cabbage and potatoes as well, and simmer partially covered for about 30 minutes, or until all the meat and vegetables and chick-peas are tender.

To serve, transfer the bird and meats to a carving board. Remove the vegetables from the broth with a slotted spoon, arrange them attractively on a large platter and mound the chick-peas in the center. Carve the chicken into suitable portions, and cut the brisket, ham and salt pork into ¼-inch slices. Arrange the chicken and meat on another heated platter and place the whole *chorizos* around them.

Traditionally, the broth is served alone as a first course, often with previously cooked fine noodles (called *cabello de ángel* or "angel's hair"). The platters of vegetables and meats then follow separately.

# Poultry and Game Birds

## Pollo a la Chilindrón
SAUTÉED CHICKEN WITH PEPPERS, TOMATOES AND OLIVES

To serve 4

A 2½- to 3-pound chicken, cut into
  6 to 8 serving pieces
Salt
Freshly ground black pepper
¼ cup olive oil
2 large onions, cut lengthwise in
  half, then into ¼-inch-wide strips
1 teaspoon finely chopped garlic
3 small sweet red or green peppers,

seeded, deribbed, and cut
  lengthwise into ¼-inch-wide strips
½ cup finely chopped *serrano* ham, or
  substitute other lean smoked ham
6 medium-sized tomatoes, peeled,
  seeded and finely chopped (*see
  huevos a la flamenca, page 68*)
6 pitted black olives, cut in half
6 pitted green olives, cut in half

Pat the chicken pieces dry with paper towels and sprinkle them liberally with salt and a few grindings of pepper. In a heavy 10- to 12-inch skillet, heat the oil over moderate heat until a light haze forms above it. Brown the chicken a few pieces at a time, starting them skin side down and turning them with tongs. Regulate the heat so that the chicken colors quickly and evenly without burning. As the pieces become a rich brown, transfer them to a plate.

Add the onions, garlic, peppers and ham to the fat remaining in the skillet. Stirring frequently, cook for 8 to 10 minutes over moderate heat until the vegetables are soft but not brown. Add the tomatoes, raise the heat and cook briskly until most of the liquid in the pan evaporates and the mixture is thick enough to hold its shape lightly in a spoon. Return the chicken to the skillet, turning the pieces about with a spoon to coat them evenly with the sauce. Then cover tightly and simmer over low heat for 25 to 30 minutes, or until the chicken is tender but not falling apart. Stir in the olives and taste for seasoning. Transfer the entire contents of the skillet to a heated serving bowl or deep platter and serve at once.

## Arroz con Pollo
CHICKEN WITH SAFFRON RICE AND PEAS

To serve 4

A 2½- to 3-pound chicken, cut into
   6 to 8 serving pieces
Salt
Freshly ground black pepper
1 tablespoon lard
¼ pound salt pork, finely diced
1 cup finely chopped onions
1 teaspoon finely chopped garlic
1 tablespoon paprika

1 cup finely chopped tomatoes
1½ cups raw medium or long-grain
   regular-milled rice or imported
   short-grain rice
1 cup fresh or frozen peas
3 cups boiling water
⅛ teaspoon ground saffron or saffron
   threads crushed with a mortar and
   pestle or with the back of a spoon
2 tablespoons finely chopped parsley

Pat the chicken pieces completely dry with paper towels and sprinkle them liberally with salt and a few grindings of pepper. In a heavy 4-quart casserole, melt the lard over moderate heat. Add the salt pork dice and, stirring frequently, cook until they have rendered all their fat and become crisp and golden brown; then, with a slotted spoon, transfer them to paper towels to drain. Add the chicken to the fat in the casserole and brown it, turning the pieces with tongs and regulating the heat so that they color quickly and evenly without burning. Set the chicken aside on a platter.

Pour off all but a thin film of fat from the casserole. Stir in the onions and garlic and cook for about 5 minutes, or until the onions are soft and transparent but not brown. Stir in the paprika, then the tomatoes and bring to a boil, stirring frequently. Cook briskly, uncovered, for about 5 minutes, or until most of the liquid in the pan evaporates and the mixture is thick enough to hold its shape lightly in a spoon.

Return the chicken and pork dice to the casserole, and add the rice, peas, boiling water, saffron and 1 teaspoon of salt. Stir together gently but thoroughly. Bring to a boil over high heat, then reduce the heat to low, cover tightly and simmer for 20 to 30 minutes, or until the chicken is tender and the rice has absorbed all the liquid. Stir in the parsley, and taste for seasoning. Cover and let stand off the heat for 5 minutes before serving directly from the casserole.

## Empanada Gallega
CHICKEN-FILLED BREAD PIE

To serve 4 to 6

BREAD DOUGH
1 package or cake of active dry or
   compressed yeast
½ teaspoon sugar
½ cup lukewarm water (110° to 115°)

2½ to 3 cups all-purpose flour
1½ teaspoons salt
½ cup lukewarm milk (110° to 115°)
1 tablespoon olive oil
1 egg, lightly beaten

In a small bowl, sprinkle the yeast and sugar over ¼ cup of the lukewarm water. Let it stand for 2 or 3 minutes, then stir to dissolve the yeast completely. Set the bowl in a warm, draft-free place, such as an unlighted oven, for 8 to 10 minutes, or until the mixture doubles in volume.

Combine 2 cups of the flour and the salt in a deep mixing bowl, make a well in the center, and pour in the yeast, milk and remaining ¼ cup of lukewarm water. Slowly stir together, adding up to 1 cup more flour, a few tablespoons at a time, until the mixture becomes a medium-firm dough that can be lifted up in a moist, solid mass.

Place the dough on a lightly floured surface and knead it by pressing down, pushing it forward several times with the heel of your hand. Fold it back on itself and knead for at least 10 minutes, or until the dough is smooth and elastic. Sprinkle a little flour over and under the dough when necessary to prevent it from sticking to the board.

Gather the dough into a ball and place it in a large, lightly buttered bowl. Dust the top with flour, drape a towel over it, and set in the warm place for 1½ hours or until the dough doubles in bulk. Punch it down with one blow of your fist, cover with a towel and let it rise again for 45 minutes.

FILLING
A 2- to 2½-pound chicken, cut into
   6 to 8 serving pieces
1 large onion, quartered
3 tablespoons olive oil
½ cup finely chopped onions
½ teaspoon finely chopped garlic
1 medium-sized sweet red or green
   pepper, deribbed, seeded and cut
   into ¼-inch squares
½ cup finely chopped *serrano* ham

or substitute prosciutto or other
   lean smoked ham
3 medium-sized tomatoes peeled,
   seeded and finely chopped *(see
   huevos a la flamenca, page 68)*, or
   substitute 1 cup chopped, drained,
   canned tomatoes
½ teaspoon salt
¼ teaspoon freshly ground black
   pepper

To prepare the filling: Place the chicken and quartered onion in a 3- to 4-quart saucepan and add enough water to cover them by 1 inch. Bring to a boil over high heat, meanwhile skimming off the foam and scum as they rise to the surface. Reduce the heat to low, cover and cook the chicken for 30 minutes or until tender but not falling apart. Transfer the chicken to a plate.

When the chicken is cool enough to handle, remove the skin with a small knife or your fingers. Cut or pull the meat away from the bones. Discard the skin and bones, and cut the chicken meat into ½-inch cubes. Set aside.

In a 10- to 12-inch skillet, heat the oil over moderate heat until a light haze forms above it. Add the onions, garlic and red or green pepper and, stirring frequently, cook for 8 to 10 minutes, or until the vegetables are soft but not brown. Stir in the ham, then add the tomatoes, raise the heat and cook briskly until most of the liquid in the pan evaporates and the mixture is thick enough to hold its shape lightly in a spoon. Add the chicken, salt and pepper, taste for seasoning and cool to room temperature.

Preheat the oven to 375°. With a pastry brush, coat a large baking sheet with 1 tablespoon of olive oil.

To assemble the pie, divide the dough into halves. On a lightly floured surface, roll each half into a circle about 12 inches in diameter and ¼-inch thick. Place one of the circles on the baking sheet and spoon the filling on top, spreading it to within about 1 inch of the outside edges. Place the second circle of dough over the filling, pressing it down firmly around the edges. Then fold up the entire rim of the pie by about ½ inch and press all around the outer edges with your fingertips or the tines of a fork to seal them securely. Let the pie rise in the warm place for about 20 minutes.

Brush the pie with the beaten egg and bake in the middle of the oven for 45 minutes, or until the top is golden. Serve hot, or at room temperature.

## *Pollo en Pepitoria*
CHICKEN BRAISED IN WHITE WINE WITH ALMONDS AND GARLIC

To serve 4 to 6

A 4- to 5-pound roasting chicken,
   cut into 6 to 8 serving pieces
Salt
White pepper
1 cup flour
½ cup olive oil
2 cups finely chopped onions
1 tablespoon finely chopped parsley
1 large bay leaf

1 cup dry white wine
2 cups water
¼ cup blanched almonds, pulverized
   in a blender or with a nut grinder
   or mortar and pestle
2 hard-cooked egg yolks
1 tablespoon finely chopped garlic
⅛ teaspoon ground saffron or saffron
   threads crushed with a mortar and
   pestle or with the back of a spoon

Pat the chicken thoroughly dry with paper towels. Sprinkle it liberally with salt and a little white pepper, dip the pieces in flour and shake them vigorously to remove the excess. In a heavy 10- to 12-inch skillet, heat the olive oil over high heat until a light haze forms above it. Starting them skin side down, brown 3 or 4 pieces of chicken at a time, turning them with tongs and regulating the heat so that the pieces color quickly and evenly without burning. Transfer them to a heavy 4- to 6-quart casserole.

Pour off all but 2 tablespoons of fat from the skillet and add the onions. Stirring frequently, cook them over moderate heat for about 5 minutes, or until they are soft and transparent but not brown. Spread the onions over the chicken in the casserole and add the parsley and bay leaf. Pour in the wine and water, and bring to a boil over high heat. Reduce the heat to low, cover tightly, and simmer, undisturbed, for 20 minutes.

With a mortar and pestle or a wooden spoon, mash the pulverized almonds, egg yolks, garlic and saffron to a smooth paste. Thin it with ¼ cup of the casserole liquid and stir the mixture gradually into the simmering casserole. Cover again, and cook for 10 minutes longer, or until the chicken is tender. With tongs, transfer the pieces to a deep, heated platter and drape it loosely with foil to keep warm.

Bring the cooking liquids to a boil over high heat and boil briskly uncovered until the sauce has reduced to about half or enough to intensify its flavor. Taste for seasoning and pour it over the chicken. Serve at once, accompanied if you like by hot boiled rice.

## *Pichones Estofados*

BRAISED SQUABS WITH CHOCOLATE SAUCE

To serve 4

4 one-pound oven-ready squabs, or
    substitute 4 one-pound partridge,
    quail, pheasant or other small
    game birds
Salt
Freshly ground black pepper
½ cup plus 1 tablespoon flour
⅓ cup olive oil
12 whole peeled white onions, each

    about 1 inch in diameter
2 medium-sized garlic cloves, peeled
    and finely sliced
¼ cup dry white wine
1 cup chicken stock, fresh or canned
2 teaspoons finely grated
    unsweetened baking chocolate
1 lemon, cut lengthwise into 8
    wedges *(optional)*

Pat the birds completely dry with paper towels, and sprinkle them liberally with salt and a few grindings of pepper. Then turn them about in ½ cup of flour and shake each one vigorously to remove the excess.

In a heavy casserole large enough to hold the birds comfortably, heat the olive oil over high heat until it splutters. Brown the birds in the oil, turning them with tongs and regulating the heat so that they color quickly and evenly on all sides without burning. Then transfer them to a plate and add the onions to the fat remaining in the casserole. Brown them over high heat, shaking the pan so that the onions roll around and color evenly. Remove them with a slotted spoon and set aside with the squabs.

Drop the garlic into the casserole and cook over moderate heat for a minute or two. Then stir in the remaining 1 tablespoon of flour. Pour in the wine and stock and, stirring constantly with a whisk, cook over high heat until the sauce comes to a boil and thickens lightly. Return the squabs to the casserole, baste them well with the sauce and cover the casserole tightly. Simmer over low heat for 40 minutes. Then add the onions, ½ teaspoon of salt and ¼ teaspoon of pepper. Cover again and simmer for 20 minutes longer, or until the onions are tender and the birds fully cooked.

With a slotted spoon, transfer the squabs to a heated platter and place the onions around them. Skim the sauce in the casserole of most of its fat and add the chocolate. Stirring constantly, cook over moderate heat for 2 or 3 minutes but do not let the chocolate boil. Taste for seasoning. Pour the sauce over the squabs and serve at once, garnished if you like with lemon.

## Arroz de Pato de Braga

ROAST DUCK WITH SAUSAGE-AND-HAM-FLAVORED RICE

To serve 4

A 5- to 6-pound oven-ready duck
1 large garlic clove, peeled and
    bruised with the side of a cleaver
    or the blade of a large, heavy
    knife
Salt
Freshly ground black pepper
2 lemons
1 cup raw medium or long-grain
    regular-milled rice, or imported
    short-grain rice
2 tablespoons lard
¼ pound Portuguese *linguiça*, or

substitute *chorizo* or any other
    garlic-seasoned smoked pork
    sausage
1 medium-sized carrot, scraped and
    finely chopped
1 medium-sized onion, finely
    chopped
¼ pound *presunto* ham, or substitute
    *serrano*, prosciutto or other lean
    smoked ham, sliced ⅛ inch thick
    and cut into 1-inch pieces
2 tablespoons fresh lemon juice
8 tablespoons finely chopped parsley

Preheat the oven to 450°. Pat the duck completely dry with paper towels. Rub the bird inside and out with the crushed garlic clove, then sprinkle the cavity liberally with salt and a few grindings of pepper.

With a small, sharp knife or a vegetable peeler with a rotating blade, remove the peel from one of the lemons without cutting through to the bitter white pith beneath it. Place the peel inside the cavity of the duck, then close the opening securely by lacing it with skewers, or by sewing it with heavy white thread.

Fasten the neck skin to the back of the duck with a skewer and truss the bird securely. Slice the peeled lemon in half crosswise and rub its cut surface over the skin of the duck.

Place the duck breast side up on a rack set in a shallow open pan. Roast undisturbed in the middle of the oven about 20 minutes, or until the duck has begun to brown. Then reduce the heat to 350° and roast about 1½ hours longer. Basting is unnecessary.

To test for doneness, pierce the thigh of the duck with the tip of a small, sharp knife. The juices should run out a pale yellow; if tinged with pink, roast another 5 to 10 minutes.

While the duck is roasting, bring 2 quarts of water to a boil over high heat in a heavy 3- to 4-quart saucepan. Pour in the rice in a thin, slow stream so that the water keeps boiling. Reduce the heat to moderate and let the rice boil uncovered for 15 minutes, or until the grains are tender but still slightly firm to the bite. Drain the rice in a colander.

Place the sausages in an 8- to 10-inch skillet and prick them in two or three places with the point of a small, sharp knife. Add enough cold water to cover them completely and bring to a boil over high heat. Then reduce the heat to low and simmer uncovered for 5 minutes. Drain on paper towels, and slice the sausage into ⅛-inch-thick rounds.

In a heavy 12-inch skillet, melt the lard over high heat until it splutters. Drop in the sausage and cook, stirring frequently, for 3 or 4 minutes. Reduce the heat to low, add the carrot and onion and, stirring frequently, cook for about 5 minutes, or until the vegetables are soft but not brown. Add the ham and cook for 2 or 3 minutes longer. With a fork stir in the rice, lemon juice, and 6 tablespoons of parsley. Taste for seasoning and set aside, covered to keep warm.

Transfer the duck to a platter and, with a large spoon, skim as much of the fat as possible from the juices remaining in the roasting pan. Pour in ½ cup of water and bring it to a boil over high heat, meanwhile scraping in any brown particles clinging to the bottom and sides of the pan. Boil briskly, stirring frequently, until the liquid thickens lightly and is reduced to about ¼ cup. Taste for seasoning.

To assemble, spread the rice mixture evenly on the bottom of a large, shallow casserole or in a deep heated platter. Carve the duck into serving pieces and arrange the pieces attractively, skin side up, on the rice. Spoon the reduced cooking liquid over the duck, sprinkle with the remaining 2 tablespoons of parsley, and garnish the casserole with the remaining lemon cut lengthwise into 8 wedges. Serve the duck and rice at once directly from the casserole.

## Perdices Estofadas

PARTRIDGES BRAISED WITH VEGETABLES AND GARLIC IN WHITE WINE

To serve 2

2 one-pound oven-ready partridges
1½ teaspoons salt
¼ teaspoon freshly ground black
   pepper
½ cup flour
2 slices lean bacon, coarsely chopped
2 tablespoons olive oil
½ cup dry white wine
1 cup water
1 small whole head of garlic,
   trimmed of root fibers and dry
   outer casing, but not peeled or

separated into individual cloves
2 whole cloves
1 small bay leaf
6 to 8 peeled white onions, each
   about 1 inch in diameter
2 medium-sized potatoes, peeled and
   cut into 1-inch cubes
3 medium-sized carrots, scraped and
   cut into 1-inch lengths
¼ cup fresh peas (¼ pound) or
   thoroughly defrosted frozen peas
1 tablespoon finely chopped parsley

Wash the partridges under cold running water and pat them completely dry with paper towels. Sprinkle them inside and out liberally with salt and a few grindings of pepper, then dip each bird in flour and shake it vigorously to remove any excess.

In a heavy 1½- to 2-quart casserole, cook the bacon in the olive oil over moderate heat, stirring occasionally, until crisp and golden. With a slotted spoon, transfer the pieces to paper towels to drain.

Heat the fat remaining in the casserole over high heat until it splutters. Add the partridges and brown them well on all sides, turning them with tongs and regulating the heat so they color quickly and evenly without burning. Transfer the birds to a plate. Pour off and discard the fat from the casserole and in its place add the wine and water. Bring to a boil over high heat, meanwhile scraping in any brown particles clinging to the bottom and sides of the casserole.

Return the partridges and bacon to the casserole and add the garlic, cloves and bay leaf. Cover tightly, reduce the heat to low and simmer undisturbed for 30 minutes. Add the onions, potatoes and carrots, cover again, and cook for 15 minutes longer. Then add the green peas and simmer covered for about 5 minutes more, or until the partridges and all of the vegetables are tender. Garnish with the parsley and serve at once, directly from the casserole, or if you prefer, transfer the partridges and vegetables to a heated platter.

# Egg Dishes

## Tortilla de Patata
POTATO AND ONION OMELET

To serve 4 to 6

1 cup plus 3 tablespoons olive oil
3 large potatoes (about 2 pounds),
   peeled and sliced into ⅛-inch-

thick rounds
2 teaspoons salt
½ cup finely chopped onions
4 eggs

In a heavy 10- to 12-inch skillet, heat 1 cup of olive oil over high heat until hot but not smoking. Add the potatoes, sprinkle them with 1 teaspoon of the salt and turn them about in the pan to coat them well with oil. Continue cooking, turning occasionally, until the potatoes brown lightly; then add the onions, reduce the heat to moderate and cook for about 10 minutes, stirring every now and then until the potatoes and onions are tender. Transfer the entire contents of the skillet to a large sieve or colander and drain the potatoes and onions of all their excess oil.

With a whisk or a rotary or electric beater, beat the eggs and the remaining 1 teaspoon of salt until frothy. Gently stir in the potatoes and onions. Heat the remaining 3 tablespoons of oil in a heavy 8-inch skillet until a light haze forms above it. Pour in the omelet mixture, spread it out with a spatula and cook over moderate heat for 2 minutes. Shake the pan periodically to keep the eggs from sticking. When the omelet is firm but not dry, cover the skillet with a flat plate and, grasping the plate and skillet firmly together, invert them and turn the omelet out in the plate. Then carefully slide the omelet back into the pan. Cook for 3 minutes longer to brown the underside, and serve at once.

NOTE: If you like, you may add previously fried chopped *chorizo* or other sausage to the omelet along with the potatoes.

## Huevos a la Flamenca

BAKED EGGS WITH VEGETABLES AND MEAT

To serve 6

NOTE: *Sofrito* (which means "lightly fried") is a basic preparation widely used in Spanish cooking. One version is the base for *huevos a la flamenca,* but a *sofrito* has many variations and is used in numerous dishes. Every *sofrito* is made with onions or garlic or both; many also include tomatoes, red or green peppers, parsley and meats such as ham or sausage; some are thickened with ground almonds, sieved hard-cooked egg yolks or even bread crumbs. Whatever the ingredients, they are generally chopped and usually cooked in olive oil.

SOFRITO

2 medium-sized tomatoes, or substitute ¾ cup chopped, drained, canned tomatoes
¼ cup olive oil
½ cup finely chopped onions
1 tablespoon finely chopped garlic
1 small sweet red or green pepper, peeled, seeded, deribbed and finely chopped
½ cup finely diced *serrano* ham, or substitute 2 ounces of prosciutto

or other lean smoked ham
1 *chorizo* sliced into ¼-inch-thick rounds, or substitute 3 ounces other garlic-seasoned smoked pork sausage
1 tablespoon finely chopped parsley
1 small bay leaf
1 teaspoon salt
¼ teaspoon freshly ground black pepper
⅓ cup water

SOFRITO: Drop the fresh tomatoes into a pan of boiling water and let them boil briskly for about 10 seconds. Run cold water over them, and with a small, sharp knife peel them. Cut out the stems, then slice the tomatoes in half crosswise. Squeeze the halves gently to remove the seeds and juices, and chop the tomatoes as fine as possible. (Canned tomatoes need only be thoroughly drained and chopped.)

In a heavy 10- to 12-inch skillet, heat the oil over moderate heat until a light haze forms above it. Add the onions, garlic and chopped pepper, and, stirring frequently, cook for 5 minutes, or until the vegetables are soft but not brown. Stir in the ham and sausage, then add the tomatoes, chopped parsley, bay leaf, salt, pepper and water, and bring to a boil. Cook briskly, uncovered, until most of the liquid in the pan has evaporated and the mixture is thick enough to hold its shape lightly in a spoon. Set aside.

EGGS

2 teaspoons olive oil
6 eggs
½ cup hot cooked fresh or frozen peas
6 hot cooked fresh or frozen asparagus tips, 3 to 4 inches long

6 to 8 strips of drained, canned pimiento, each about 3 inches long and ¼ inch wide
3 tablespoons pale dry sherry
Parsley sprigs (optional)

EGGS: Preheat the oven to 400°. Using a pastry brush, coat the bottom and sides of a 9-by-9-by-2-inch baking dish with the 2 teaspoons of oil. Discard the bay leaf and spread the *sofrito* evenly in the dish. One at a time, break the eggs into the dish, arranging them in a circle on top of the *sofrito*. Or break the eggs into a saucer and slide them gently into the dish.

Heap the peas in three or four mounds on the *sofrito* and arrange the asparagus in parallel rows, draping the pimiento strips decoratively over them. Sprinkle the eggs and vegetables with sherry, cover the dish, and bake in the middle of the oven for 20 minutes, or until an opaque film has formed over the egg yolks and the whites are firm. Serve at once, garnished with parsley.

HOW TO PEEL PEPPERS: Impale the pepper on the tines of a long-handled fork and turn it over a gas flame until the skin blisters and darkens. Or place it on a baking sheet and broil it 3 inches from the heat for about 5 minutes, turning it so all sides color evenly. Wrap the pepper in a damp towel, let it rest for a few minutes, then rub it with the towel until the skin slips off. Cut out the stem and white membranes or ribs, and discard the seeds.

## *Ervilhas Guisadas à Portuguêsa*
PEAS PORTUGUESE

To serve 2 to 4

2 tablespoons butter
½ cup finely chopped onions
¾ cup chicken stock, fresh or canned
3 cups cooked fresh green peas
  (about 3 pounds), or substitute 3
  ten-ounce packages frozen peas,
  thoroughly defrosted but not cooked
¼ cup finely chopped parsley

¼ cup finely chopped fresh coriander
  leaves (cilantro)
½ teaspoon sugar
Salt
Freshly ground black pepper
4 ounces *linguiça* or *chorizo* (or
  substitute other garlic-seasoned
  smoked pork sausage),
  cut into ¼ inch slices
4 eggs

In a heavy 10-inch skillet or shallow flameproof casserole, melt the butter over moderate heat. When the foam has almost subsided, add the onions and, stirring frequently, cook for 8 to 10 minutes, or until they are lightly colored. Stir in the stock, freshly cooked or frozen peas, parsley, coriander, sugar, ¼ teaspoon of salt and a few grindings of pepper and overlap the sausage slices around the edge of the skillet. Bring to a boil over high heat, then reduce the heat to low, cover and simmer for 5 minutes.

Break 1 egg into a saucer and, holding the dish close to the pan, slide the egg on top of the peas. One at a time, slide the other eggs into the pan, keeping them well apart. Sprinkle them lightly with salt and pepper. Cover the skillet and cook for 3 or 4 minutes until the egg yolks are covered with an opaque film and the whites are set. Serve at once, directly from the skillet.

# Vegetables, Rice, Salads and Sauces

## Coliflor al Ajo Arriero

DEEP FRIED CAULIFLOWER WITH GARLIC AND VINEGAR SAUCE

To serve 4 to 6

A 1- to 1½-pound head of
   cauliflower, trimmed and separated
   into florets
Salt
Vegetable oil or shortening for deep
   frying
White pepper
½ cup flour
2 eggs, lightly beaten
¾ cup soft fresh crumbs made from

French or Italian bread, trimmed
   of crusts and pulverized in a
   blender or pulled apart with a
   fork
6 tablespoons olive oil
2 garlic cloves, peeled and lightly
   bruised with the flat of a knife
1 tablespoon paprika
2 tablespoons white vinegar
3 tablespoons boiling water

Drop the cauliflower florets into enough lightly salted boiling water to cover them by at least 1 inch. Cook briskly uncovered for 8 to 10 minutes, or until the cauliflower shows only the slightest resistance when pierced with the point of a small, sharp knife. Drain on paper towels.

Heat 3 to 4 inches of vegetable oil or shortening in a deep-fat fryer or large, heavy saucepan until it reaches 350° on a deep-frying thermometer. Sprinkle the florets liberally with salt and a little white pepper, dip them in the flour and shake vigorously to remove the excess. Then dip them in the beaten eggs and into the crumbs. Turning them with tongs, deep-fry the florets (in two batches if necessary) for about 4 minutes, or until they are golden brown. Drain on paper towels. Then arrange them on a heated platter and drape with foil to keep them warm.

In a 6- to 8-inch skillet, heat the 6 tablespoons of olive oil over low heat until a light haze forms above it. Drop in the garlic cloves and, stirring constantly, cook for 2 or 3 minutes. Then remove them with a slotted spoon. Add the paprika, vinegar and water to the oil and, stirring constantly, cook for a minute or so. Then pour over the cauliflower, turn the florets about with a spoon to coat them evenly and serve at once.

## Espinacas con Piñones y Almendras
SPINACH WITH PINE NUTS AND ALMONDS

To serve 4

¼ cup olive oil
1 large garlic clove, peeled and cut
in half lengthwise
¼ cup pine nuts (pignoli)
¼ cup blanched slivered almonds
1 pound freshly cooked spinach,

drained and finely chopped, or 2
ten-ounce packages chopped
frozen spinach, thoroughly
defrosted and drained
¼ cup finely diced serrano ham or
substitute 1 ounce prosciutto or
other lean smoked ham
1 teaspoon salt

In a heavy 10- to 12-inch skillet, heat the olive oil over moderate heat until a light haze forms above it. Add the garlic and, stirring constantly, cook for 1 or 2 minutes. Remove the garlic with a slotted spoon and discard it. Add the pine nuts and almonds to the oil remaining in the pan and cook for 2 or 3 minutes, or until they are slightly brown. Add the spinach, ham and salt and toss together with a spoon until the ingredients are thoroughly mixed and heated through. Taste for seasoning and serve at once.

## Judías Verdes con Salsa de Tomate
GREEN BEANS IN TOMATO SAUCE

To serve 4

1 teaspoon salt
1 pound fresh green string beans,
trimmed and cut into 2-inch lengths
2 tablespoons olive oil
¼ cup finely chopped onions
1 teaspoon finely chopped garlic

4 medium-sized tomatoes, peeled,
seeded and finely chopped (see
huevos a la flamenca, page 68), or
substitute 1½ cups chopped,
drained, canned tomatoes
1 tablespoon finely chopped parsley
2 teaspoons sugar
Freshly ground black pepper

In a heavy 3- to 4-quart saucepan, bring the salt and 2 quarts of water to a boil over high heat. Drop in the beans, a handful at a time. Bring to a boil again, reduce the heat to moderate and boil uncovered for 10 to 15 minutes until the beans are barely tender. Drain in a colander and set the beans aside.

Heat the olive oil in a heavy 10- to 12-inch skillet until a light haze forms above it. Add the onions and garlic and, stirring frequently, cook over moderate heat for 5 minutes, or until the onions are soft and transparent but not brown. Stir in the tomatoes, parsley, sugar and a few grindings of pepper, bring to a boil, and cook, uncovered, until most of the liquid evaporates and the mixture is thick enough to hold its shape lightly in a spoon.

Stir in the beans and simmer for a minute or two until they are heated through. Taste for seasoning and serve at once from a heated bowl.

## Habas a la Catalana
FAVA BEANS WITH SAUSAGES AND MINT

To serve 4 to 6

1 pound *chorizos,* or other garlic-
 seasoned smoked pork sausage
1 tablespoon lard
¼ pound salt pork, finely diced
½ cup finely chopped scallions
1 teaspoon finely chopped garlic
½ cup dry white wine
½ cup water

1 tablespoon finely cut fresh mint
1 small bay leaf, crumbled
½ teaspoon salt
Freshly ground black pepper
4 cups cooked, fresh fava beans or
 substitute drained, canned favas
 or frozen baby lima beans
2 tablespoons finely chopped parsley

Place the sausages in an 8- to 10-inch skillet and prick them in two or three places with the point of a small, sharp knife. Add enough cold water to cover them completely and bring to a boil over high heat. Reduce the heat to low and simmer uncovered for 5 minutes. Drain on paper towels, then slice the sausages into ¼-inch-thick rounds.

In a heavy 3- to 4-quart casserole, melt the lard over moderate heat. Add the salt pork and, stirring frequently, cook until the pieces have rendered all their fat and become crisp and golden brown. With a slotted spoon, transfer them to paper towels to drain.

Add the scallions and garlic to the fat in the pan and cook for about 5 minutes, or until the scallions are soft but not brown. Pour in the wine and water and add the sliced sausages, pork dice, mint, bay leaf, salt and a few grindings of pepper. Bring to a boil over high heat, reduce the heat to low and simmer partially covered for 20 minutes.

Add the beans and parsley and simmer uncovered, stirring frequently, for about 10 minutes longer, or until the beans are heated through.

Taste the *habas a la catalana* for seasoning and serve at once from a heated bowl or a deep heated platter.

## Batatas à Portuguêsa
PORTUGUESE FRIED POTATOES

To serve 4

3 tablespoons butter
3 tablespoons olive oil
1½ pounds new potatoes, peeled

and sliced into ¼-inch-thick rounds
½ teaspoon salt
Freshly ground black pepper
1 tablespoon finely chopped parsley

In a heavy 10- to 12-inch skillet, melt the butter in the olive oil over moderate heat. When the foam begins to subside, add the potatoes. Turning them frequently with a metal spatula, cook for 15 minutes or until they are tender and golden brown. Season with salt and a few grindings of pepper, then transfer the potatoes to a heated bowl or platter and serve at once, sprinkled with parsley if you like. When fried potatoes accompany *iscas (Recipe Index)* or *bife à portuguêsa (Recipe Index),* they are traditionally arranged in a symmetrical ring around the meat.

## Patatas en Salsa Verde
POTATOES IN PARSLEY SAUCE

To serve 4 to 6

5 tablespoons olive oil
6 small boiling potatoes (about 2
   pounds), peeled and sliced
   crosswise into ½-inch rounds
½ cup finely chopped onions

1 teaspoon finely chopped garlic
2 tablespoons finely chopped parsley
1 teaspoon salt
¼ teaspoon freshly ground black
   pepper
1½ cups boiling water

In a heavy 10- to 12-inch skillet, heat the olive oil over high heat until a light haze forms above it. Add the potatoes. Turning them frequently with a metal spatula, cook for 10 minutes, or until they are a light golden brown on all sides.

Scatter the onions, garlic, parsley, salt and pepper on top of the potatoes and pour in the boiling water. Do not stir. Instead, shake the pan back and forth for a minute or two to distribute the water evenly.

Cover the skillet tightly and simmer over low heat for about 20 minutes, or until the potatoes are tender but not falling apart. Shake the skillet back and forth occasionally to prevent the potatoes from sticking to the pan.

With a slotted spatula transfer the potatoes to a platter and pour a few teaspoonfuls of their cooking liquid over them. Serve the remaining liquid separately in a sauceboat.

## Arroz con Azafrán
SAFFRON RICE

To serve 4 to 6

2 tablespoons olive oil
2 tablespoons finely chopped onions
1½ cups raw long-grain rice
3 cups boiling water

1½ teaspoons salt
⅛ teaspoon ground saffron, or
 saffron threads pulverized with a
 mortar and pestle or with the back
 of a spoon

In a heavy 10- to 12-inch skillet, heat the oil over moderate heat until a light haze forms above it. Add the onions and, stirring frequently, cook for 5 minutes, or until they are soft and transparent but not brown. Pour in the rice and stir for 2 or 3 minutes to coat the grains well with oil. Do not let the rice brown. Add the water, salt and saffron, and bring to a boil, still stirring. Cover the pan tightly and reduce the heat to its lowest point. Simmer undisturbed for 20 minutes, or until all the liquid has been absorbed by the rice and the grains are tender but not too soft.

Fluff the rice with a fork before serving and taste for seasoning. If the rice must wait, drape the pan with a towel and keep it warm in a preheated 200° oven. *Arroz con azafrán* may be served with *riñones al Jerez, zarzuela de mariscos* and *mariscos a la Costa Brava (all in Recipe Index)*.


## Legumbres Rellenas
STUFFED VEGETABLES

To serve 4

SOFRITO
¼ cup olive oil
½ cup finely chopped onions
½ teaspoon finely chopped garlic
¼ cup finely chopped green pepper
2 tablespoons flour
2 medium-sized tomatoes, peeled,

seeded and finely chopped *(see
huevos a la flamenca, page 68)*, or
 substitute ⅔ cup chopped,
 drained, canned tomatoes
1 cup water
2 teaspoons salt
½ cup dry white wine

For the *sofrito*, heat the olive oil in a heavy 8- to 10-inch skillet until a light haze forms above it. Add the chopped onions, chopped garlic and chopped pepper and, stirring frequently, cook over moderate heat for 5 minutes, or until the vegetables are soft but not brown. Stir in the flour and cook for a minute or so. Then add the tomatoes, water and salt and bring to a boil over high heat. Reduce the heat to low and simmer for about 10 minutes, stirring occasionally. Purée the mixture in a food mill or use the back of a large spoon to rub it through a fine sieve set over a bowl. Stir in the wine, taste for seasoning, and set aside.

STUFFING

1½ pounds lean boneless veal, finely ground

¼ pound *serrano* ham including some of the fat, cut into 1-inch cubes, or substitute prosciutto or other smoked ham

1 medium-sized onion, peeled and quartered

2 medium-sized garlic cloves, peeled

4 parsley sprigs

For the stuffing, put the veal, ham, quartered onion, garlic cloves and parsley through the finest blade of a meat grinder. Beat the mixture vigorously until the ingredients are thoroughly blended. (To make the stuffing by hand, chop the ham, onion, garlic and parsley as fine as possible and beat them together with the veal until thoroughly blended.)

VEGETABLES

4 firm ripe tomatoes, each about 2½ inches in diameter

4 small sweet red or green peppers, each about 2½ inches in diameter

2 large zucchini or other green summer squash, each about 2½ inches in diameter and 6 to 8 inches long

4 small potatoes, each about 2½ inches in diameter

Cut a ¼-inch slice off the stem ends of the tomatoes and hollow each one out with a small spoon. Sprinkle their cavities lightly with salt and turn the tomatoes upside down on paper towels to drain for at least 10 minutes. Then gently pat the cavities dry with paper towels. Cut a ¼-inch slice off the top of each pepper, remove the seeds and cut out the white ribs.

Peel the zucchini and potatoes, and cut the zucchini crosswise into 2-inch-long rounds. With a small spoon scoop out the top of each zucchini cylinder to make a boatlike shell about ½ inch thick and hollow out each of the potatoes in a similar fashion. Place the potatoes in cold water to prevent them from discoloring.

Preheat the oven to 400°. Fill the vegetables with the stuffing mixture, patting it in firmly. Arrange the peppers, squash and potatoes side by side on the bottom of a shallow baking dish, large enough to hold all the vegetables comfortably in one layer. (Leave space for the tomatoes. Because they take less time to cook, they will be added later.) Pour the *sofrito* over the vegetables, cover the dish tightly with its lid or a piece of foil, and bake in the middle of the oven for 45 minutes. Then add the tomatoes, re-cover the dish, and bake for 15 minutes longer, or until all the vegetables are tender. Serve at once, directly from the baking dish.

# Menestra de Legumbres
MIXED VEGETABLE CASSEROLE

To serve 6 to 8

SAUCE

¼ cup olive oil
1 cup finely chopped onions
½ teaspoon finely chopped garlic
3 ounces *serrano* ham cut into ½-
    inch squares, or substitute
    prosciutto or other lean smoked ham

2 tablespoons flour
1½ cups fresh or canned chicken
    stock or water
1 teaspoon salt
¼ teaspoon freshly ground black
    pepper

Preheat the oven to 350°. In a heavy 8- to 10-inch skillet, heat ¼ cup of olive oil over moderate heat until a light haze forms above it. Add the onions and garlic and, stirring frequently, cook for 5 minutes, or until the onions are soft and transparent but not brown. Add the ham and cook 2 minutes longer. Stir in the 2 tablespoons of flour and add the chicken stock or water, salt and pepper. Mix thoroughly, and simmer uncovered for about 5 minutes, or until the mixture comes to a boil and thickens. Set aside.

VEGETABLES

½ to ¾ cup olive oil
1 nine-ounce box frozen artichoke
    hearts, thoroughly defrosted
2 eggs, lightly beaten
1½ cups flour
1 medium-sized cauliflower (about
    1 pound), trimmed and separated
    into individual florets
2 medium-sized potatoes, peeled and
    cut into strips 2 inches long, ½
    inch wide and ½ inch thick
2 medium-sized carrots, scraped and

cut into thin strips about 2 inches
    long
½ pound fresh asparagus, trimmed
    and cut into 2-inch lengths
½ pound green or wax string beans,
    or a mixture of beans, trimmed
    and cut into 2-inch lengths
¼ pound mushrooms, trimmed and
    cut into quarters
½ cup (½ pound) fresh peas or
    substitute frozen peas, thoroughly
    defrosted

Heat another ¼ cup of oil in a heavy 12-inch skillet until it is quite hot but not smoking. With tongs, dip the artichoke hearts, one at a time, into the eggs and then into the 1½ cups of flour. Drop them into the skillet and cook over moderate heat, turning the artichokes frequently and regulating the heat so that they brown quickly and evenly without burning. Transfer them to a double thickness of paper towels to drain. In a similar fashion, coat the cauliflower pieces with the egg and flour and brown them in the fat remaining in the pan. Add more oil to the skillet, 1 or 2 tablespoons at a time, as necessary. Drain on paper towels.

Pour ¼ cup of the remaining olive oil into the skillet and heat it over moderate heat until a light haze forms above it. Add the potatoes and carrots and, turning them frequently with a broad metal spatula, cook for about 5 minutes, or until they are light brown.

To assemble the *menestra:* arrange the artichoke hearts and cauliflower on the bottom of a heavy 4- to 5-quart casserole. Sprinkle liberally with salt. Place the asparagus spears on top, then arrange the beans and mushrooms in individual layers. Sprinkle with salt again. Scatter the potatoes and carrots evenly on top and cover them with the sauce, spreading it out with a rubber spatula. Cover tightly and bake in the middle of the oven for 30 minutes. Add the peas to the casserole, cover again, and bake for 10 minutes longer. Serve at once, directly from the casserole.

## Pisto Manchego
STEWED PEPPERS, TOMATOES, SQUASH AND ONIONS

To serve 4

⅓ cup olive oil
3 cups coarsely chopped onions
2 medium-sized zucchini, scrubbed
    and cut into ¼-inch cubes
2 large green peppers, deribbed,
    seeded and coarsely chopped
2 teaspoons salt

4 medium-sized tomatoes, peeled,
    seeded and coarsely chopped *(see
    huevos a la flamenca, page 68)*
1 egg, lightly beaten

1 hard-cooked egg, the white cut
    lengthwise into ¼-inch strips and
    the yolk crumbled (optional)

In a heavy 12-inch skillet, heat the olive oil over high heat until a light haze forms above it. Add the onions, squash, peppers and salt, stir together, then cover the pan, and reduce the heat to its lowest possible point. Cook for about 40 minutes, or until the vegetables are tender, stirring occasionally.

Meanwhile, place the tomatoes in a 1- to 1½-quart saucepan and bring to a boil over moderate heat. Stirring and mashing them against the sides of the pan, cook briskly uncovered until most of the liquid in the pan evaporates and the tomatoes become a thick, fairly smooth purée.

Stir them into the vegetables, then pour in the beaten egg, stirring constantly. Simmer about 10 seconds but do not let the mixture boil. Taste for seasoning and serve at once. Garnish the top, if you like, with the hard-cooked egg. *Pisto* is usually served as an accompaniment to roasted meat.

## Uma Salada Portuguêsa

MIXED GREEN SALAD

To serve 2

¼ cup olive oil
¼ cup fresh lemon juice
Salt, preferably coarse salt
Freshly ground black pepper
1 head Boston, bibb, or Romaine
    lettuce plus 2 or 3 chickory leaves,

cut into small pieces
1 bunch water cress
1 large tomato, thinly sliced
1 large red onion, thinly sliced and
    separated into rings
8 ripe olives, optional

Beat the oil and lemon juice together with a fork or whisk until they are well blended. Season liberally with salt and a few grindings of pepper.

Gently toss the lettuce and water cress together with the dressing and arrange the greens attractively on a large chilled serving plate. Place the tomato slices slightly overlapping on top and arrange the onion rings (and olives if you are using them) around them. Serve at once.

## Ali-oli

GARLIC MAYONNAISE

To make about 2 cups

4 to 8 medium-sized garlic cloves,
    peeled and coarsely chopped
¼ teaspoon salt

1 tablespoon fresh lemon juice
2 egg yolks
1½ cups olive oil
1 to 2 tablespoons cold water

With a mortar and pestle or with the back of a wooden spoon, vigorously mash the garlic, salt and lemon juice to a smooth paste. Beat in the egg yolks, one at a time, continuing to beat until the mixture is thick. Now transfer it to a mixing bowl and with a whisk or a rotary or electric beater, beat in the oil, ½ teaspoon at a time; make sure each ½ teaspoon is absorbed before adding more. When about ½ cup of oil has been beaten in, the sauce should have thickened to a thick cream. Add the remaining oil by teaspoonfuls, beating constantly. If the mayonnaise becomes too thick to beat easily, thin it from time to time with 1 teaspoon of cold water, using up to 2 tablespoons if necessary. The finished sauce should be thick enough to hold its shape solidly in a spoon. Taste for seasoning.

*Ali-oli* is traditionally served, from a separate bowl or sauceboat, as an accompaniment to grilled or boiled meats and fish.

## Romescu

ALMOND AND HOT PEPPER SAUCE

To make about 1½ cups

¼ cup blanched slivered almonds
1 teaspoon finely chopped garlic
½ teaspoon cayenne pepper
1 teaspoon salt

1 small tomato, peeled, seeded and
finely chopped *(see huevos a la
flamenca, page 68)*
¼ cup red wine vinegar
1 cup olive oil

Preheat the oven to 350°. Place the almonds on a baking sheet and toast them in the middle of the oven for about 10 minutes, or until they color lightly. Then pulverize them in an electric blender or with a nut grinder or mortar and pestle.

Crush the almonds, garlic, cayenne pepper and salt together with a large mortar and pestle or in a small bowl with the back of a large spoon. Add the tomato and vinegar and mash the mixture vigorously to a smooth paste.

Then transfer it to a mixing bowl and, with a whisk or a rotary or electric beater, beat in the oil a teaspoon at a time. Make sure each teaspoon is absorbed before adding more. When about ½ cup of the oil has been beaten in, the sauce should be thick and creamy. Beating constantly, pour in the remaining oil in a slow thin stream.

The finished sauce should be thick enough to hold its shape almost solidly in a spoon. Taste for seasoning and serve with grilled or boiled meats, shellfish or fish.

NOTE: In Catalonia *romescu* is often served with a bowl of *ali-oli (opposite)*, and the two are then combined to taste at the table.

# Breads, Grullers and Gookies

## Bôlo Rei

CANDIED FRUIT AND NUT BREAD

To make two 10-inch rings

2 packages or cakes of active dry or
    compressed yeast
A pinch plus 1 cup sugar
¼ cup lukewarm water (110° to 115°)
5 to 6 cups all-purpose flour
1 teaspoon salt
1 cup lukewarm milk (110° to 115°)
3 eggs
¼ pound (1 stick) unsalted butter
    cut into small bits
3 tablespoons seedless raisins
3 tablespoons finely diced mixed
    candied fruit peel

3 tablespoons blanched, toasted, and
    coarsely chopped almonds *(see bôlo
    de amêndoa à algarvia, page 98)*
2 tablespoons butter, softened
1 egg, lightly beaten
Crystallized fruits, whole blanched
    and toasted almonds *(see bôlo de
    amêndoa à algarvia, page 98)* and
    whole pine nuts *(pignoli)* for
    garnish
½ cup coarsely granulated
    decorating sugar or substitute
    regular granulated sugar

In a small shallow bowl, sprinkle the yeast and a pinch of sugar over the lukewarm water. Let the mixture stand for 2 or 3 minutes, then stir to dissolve
the yeast completely. Set the bowl in a warm draft-free place, such as an un
lighted oven, for 5 to 8 minutes, or until the yeast has doubled in volume.

    In a deep mixing bowl, combine the 1 cup of sugar, 4 cups of the flour
and the salt. Make a well in the center and pour in the yeast and milk. Drop
in the eggs, gently stir together with a large spoon, then beat until the ingredients are well combined. Beat in the ¼ pound of butter, then add up to
2 cups more flour, beating it in ¼ cup at a time, and using as much as necessary to form a dough that can be gathered into a soft ball. When the
dough becomes difficult to stir easily, work in the flour with your fingers.

    Place the dough on a lightly floured surface, and knead it by pressing it
down, pushing it forward several times with the heel of your hand and folding it back on itself. Repeat for about 15 minutes, or until the dough is
smooth and elastic. Sprinkle it from time to time with a little flour to prevent it from sticking to the board.

Lightly knead in the raisins, candied fruit peel and almonds. Shape the dough into a ball and place it in a lightly buttered bowl. Drape loosely with a kitchen towel and set aside in a warm, draft-free place for 1 hour, or until the dough doubles in bulk.

With a pastry brush coat the bottom and sides of 2 large baking sheets with 2 tablespoons of softened butter. Punch the dough down with a single blow of your fist, let it rest for 10 minutes, then divide it in two. Form each half into a round loaf and with your fingertips press a hole in the center of each loaf and push the dough into a ring about 8 inches in diameter. The hole in the center should be about 4 inches across. Place a loaf on each baking sheet. To insure that the rings hold their shape, butter the outside of 2 ovenproof baking dishes 3 to 4 inches in diameter, invert and set one in the center of each loaf. Let the bread rise in the warm place for 30 minutes.

Meanwhile, preheat the oven to 350°. With a pastry brush, coat the entire surface of the bread with beaten egg. Then decorate the tops and sides of the rings with the crystallized fruits, whole almonds and pine nuts, pressing them lightly into the dough and arranging them as fancifully as you like. Sprinkle with the ½ cup of decorating sugar and bake in the middle of the oven for about an hour, or until golden brown and crusty. The bread may be served warm or it may be cooled to room temperature on a rack.

## Massa Sovada
PORTUGUESE SWEET BREAD

To make two 9-inch round loaves

2 packages or cakes of active dry or
   compressed yeast
A pinch plus 1 cup sugar
¼ cup lukewarm water (110° to 115°)
5 to 6 cups all-purpose flour
1 teaspoon salt

1 cup lukewarm milk (110° to 115°)
3 eggs
¼ pound (1 stick) unsalted butter,
   cut into small bits
2 tablespoons softened butter
1 egg, lightly beaten

In a small bowl, sprinkle the yeast and a pinch of sugar over the lukewarm water. Let the mixture stand for 2 or 3 minutes, then stir to dissolve the yeast completely. Set the bowl in a warm, draft-free place, such as an unlighted oven, for 5 to 8 minutes, or until the mixture doubles in volume.

In a deep mixing bowl, combine the 1 cup of sugar, 4 cups of the flour and the salt. Make a well in the center, pour in the yeast and milk, and drop in the eggs. Gently stir together with a large spoon, then beat vigorously until all the ingredients are well combined. Beat in ¼ pound of butter, then add up to 2 cups more flour, beating it in ¼ cup at a time, and using as much as necessary to form a dough that can be gathered into a soft ball. If the dough becomes difficult to stir, work in the flour with your fingers.

Place the dough on a lightly floured surface, and knead it, pressing down and pushing it forward several times with the heel of your hand. Fold it back on itself and repeat for about 15 minutes until it is smooth and elastic.

Shape the dough into a ball and place it in a large, lightly buttered bowl. Dust the top with flour, drape with a towel and set aside in the warm, draft-free place for 45 minutes to an hour until the dough doubles in bulk.

With a pastry brush, coat the bottom and sides of two 9-inch pie plates with 2 tablespoons of softened butter. Punch the dough down with a single blow of your fist, then transfer it to a lightly floured surface and let it rest for 10 minutes. Divide the dough in two and pat the halves into flattened round loaves about 8 inches across. Place them in the pie plates and let them rise in a warm place for about 40 minutes.

Preheat the oven to 350°. With a pastry brush, coat the top of both loaves with beaten egg. Bake in the middle of the oven for about 1 hour, or until the loaves are golden brown and crusty. Cool on cake racks.

NOTE: The same dough is often shaped into snail-like loaves (*caracois*) or braids (*trança à tricana*). To make the *caracois*, divide the dough into two equal parts and roll each part into a long rope about 1½ inches in diameter. One at a time, loop a rope in ever-smaller concentric circles inside a 9-inch round pie plate to fill the pan completely. Let the loaves rise for 40 minutes, brush with beaten egg and set a few raisins in the center before baking.

For the trança à tricana, gently incorporate ¼ cup of dried currants into the dough after the first kneading. Let the dough rise for an hour. Then punch it down, let it rest 10 minutes and divide the dough in two. Roll each half into three 14-inch-long ropes. Lay three ropes side by side and gently interweave them into a thick braid, turning the ends under slightly to smooth and seal them. Make the second braid similarly, then carefully place the loaves on buttered baking sheets and let them rise for 40 minutes. Brush the braids with beaten egg and sprinkle them with ½ cup of sugar (preferably coarsely granulated decorating sugar) before baking them.

## Broa
PORTUGUESE CORNBREAD

To make one 9-inch round loaf

| | |
|---|---|
| 1½ cups yellow cornmeal, pulverized in a blender until fine | 1 package or cake of active dry or compressed yeast |
| 1½ teaspoons salt | 1 teaspoon sugar |
| 1 cup boiling water | ¼ cup lukewarm water (110° to 115°) |
| 1 tablespoon plus 1 teaspoon olive oil | 1¾ to 2 cups all-purpose flour |

In a large mixing bowl combine 1 cup of the cornmeal, the salt and boiling water and stir vigorously until smooth. Stir in 1 tablespoon of the olive oil, then cool to lukewarm. In a small bowl, sprinkle the yeast and sugar over the lukewarm water. Let it stand for 2 or 3 minutes, then stir to dissolve the yeast completely. Set the bowl in a warm draft-free place, such as an unlighted oven, for 8 to 10 minutes, or until the yeast doubles in volume.

Stir the yeast into the cornmeal mixture. Stirring constantly, gradually add the remaining ½ cup of cornmeal and 1 cup of the flour. Gather the dough into a ball, place it in a bowl and drape a towel over it. Set it aside in the draft-free place for about 30 minutes, or until it doubles in bulk.

With a pastry brush, coat the bottom and sides of a 9-inch pie pan with the remaining 1 teaspoon of olive oil. Turn the dough out on a lightly floured surface and punch it down. Then knead it by pressing it down with the heel of your hand, pushing it forward and folding it back on itself repeatedly for about 5 minutes, meanwhile adding up to 1 cup more flour to make a firm but not stiff dough. Pat and shape it into a round flat loaf and place it in the greased pan. Drape a towel over it and set it aside in the draft-free place for about 30 minutes, or until it doubles in bulk again.

Preheat the oven to 350°. Bake the bread in the middle of the oven for 40 minutes, or until the top is golden. Transfer it to a rack to cool. *Broa* is served with *ervilhas guisadas à portuguêsa (page 69)* and *caldo verde (page 12)*.

## Mantecadas de Astorga
CINNAMON MUFFINS

To make about 20

½ pound (2 sticks) unsalted butter,
  softened
1 cup sugar

1½ cups all-purpose flour
6 eggs
1 tablespoon ground cinnamon

Preheat the oven to 350°. Line the cups of two 12-cup muffin tins with paper cupcake liners. The cups should measure about 2½ inches in diameter across the bottom.

With an electric mixer, beat the butter, sugar and 2 tablespoons of the flour together until the mixture is light and fluffy. Then beat in the eggs, one at a time. Combine the remaining flour and the cinnamon and sift them slowly over the mixture, beating all the while. Continue to beat until the batter is smooth. (To make the batter by hand, cream the butter, sugar and 2 tablespoons of the flour together by mashing and beating them against the side of the bowl with a large spoon until fluffy. Beat in the eggs, one at a time. Then combine the remaining flour and the cinnamon and gradually sift them into the batter, beating well after each addition.)

Ladle the batter into the paper-lined muffin cups, filling each one about half full. Bake in the middle of the oven for 15 minutes, or until the tops of the muffins are golden brown and firm to the touch. Carefully turn the muffins out of the tins and serve warm or at room temperature.

## Churros Madrileños
CRISP-FRIED CRULLERS

To make 12 to 15

2 cups water
1 teaspoon salt
2 cups all-purpose flour

Vegetable oil or shortening for deep-
  fat frying
Sugar

In a heavy 2- to 3-quart saucepan, bring the water and salt to a boil over high heat. Immediately remove the pan from the heat and pour in the flour all at once. Beat vigorously with a wooden spoon until the mixture forms a thick coarse paste that pulls away from the sides of the pan in a mass. Cool to room temperature.

Heat 2 to 3 inches of oil or shortening in a deep-fat fryer or large, heavy skillet until it is very hot but not smoking, or until it reaches a temperature of 400° on a deep-frying thermometer.

Spoon about half of the dough into a large metal cookie press fitted with a star disc, and press three or four 6-inch-long ribbons of dough directly into the hot fat, cutting the ribbons off at the tip with a small knife as you proceed. Turning the crullers occasionally, fry them for 5 to 8 minutes, or until they are a rich golden brown on all sides. Using kitchen tongs, transfer the browned crullers to a double thickness of paper towels to drain while you fry the rest.

Serve the crullers while they are still warm. Just before serving, sprinkle them liberally with sugar.

NOTE: Do not try to force the *churros* paste through a pastry bag—the mixture is so stiff it must be shaped with a cookie press or, if you can find it, one of the special *churros* makers used in Spain.

## Tortas de Aceite
ANISE- AND SESAME-SEED COOKIES

To make 12 3-inch cookies

| | |
|---|---|
| 1 cup olive oil or vegetable oil | 1 teaspoon finely grated lemon peel |
| A strip of lemon peel 2 inches long and ½ inch wide | 1 teaspoon finely grated orange peel |
| | ⅓ cup sugar |
| 2 teaspoons anise seeds | 2¼ cups all-purpose flour |
| 2 teaspoons sesame seeds | 1 tablespoon ground cinnamon |
| ½ cup dry white wine | ¼ cup blanched, sliced almonds |

In a small saucepan or skillet, heat the oil over moderate heat until a light haze forms above it. Remove the pan from the heat, stir in the strip of lemon peel and the anise and sesame seeds, and then set the oil aside to cool to room temperature.

Discard the lemon peel and pour the oil and seeds into a large mixing bowl. Stir in the wine, grated lemon peel and orange peel, and the sugar, and mix until the sugar dissolves. Sift the flour and cinnamon into the mixture, ½ cup or so at a time, stirring well after each addition. When the dough becomes too stiff to stir easily with a spoon, knead in the remaining flour with your hands. Gather the dough into a ball and let it rest at room temperature for at least 30 minutes.

Preheat the oven to 400°. Divide the dough into 12 equal pieces. Pat and shape each piece into a flat cookie about 3 inches in diameter and ½ inch thick. Arrange the cookies about 2 inches apart on an ungreased baking sheet. Press 6 to 8 almond slices gently but firmly into the top of each cookie and bake in the middle of the oven for about 40 minutes, or until the tops of the cookies are firm to the touch. Transfer them to a rack to cool. The cookies may be kept for 2 or 3 weeks in a tightly covered jar or tin.

## Bizcocho Genovesa

LADYFINGERS

To make about 24 four-inch-long ladyfingers

| | |
|---|---|
| 2 tablespoons butter, softened | measuring |
| ¼ cup flour | 1 teaspoon double-acting baking |
| 2 eggs | powder |
| 5 egg yolks | 1 teaspoon vanilla extract |
| ½ cup sugar | ¼ teaspoon finely grated lemon peel |
| 1 cup all-purpose flour, sifted before | ½ cup confectioners' sugar, sifted |

Preheat the oven to 450°. With a pastry brush or paper towel, coat the bottom and sides of two 12-mold ladyfinger tins or 2 large baking sheets with the softened butter. Sprinkle the ¼ cup of flour into the pans and tip them from side to side to spread it evenly. Then invert the pans and rap them sharply on a table to remove the excess flour.

Warm a large mixing bowl in hot water and dry it quickly but thoroughly. Drop in the eggs and egg yolks, add the sugar and beat with a whisk or a rotary or electric beater until the mixture is thick, pale yellow and has almost tripled in volume. With an electric mixer, this will take 10 to 15 minutes; with a whisk or rotary beater, it may take as long as 25 or 30 minutes.

Sift the flour and baking powder over the eggs a little at a time, gently but thoroughly folding them together with a rubber spatula as you proceed. When all the flour has been absorbed fold in the vanilla and lemon peel.

Scoop the batter into a large pastry bag fitted with a ½-inch plain tip and pipe it into the molds or onto the baking sheets in strips about 3½ inches long and 2 inches apart. Sprinkle the ladyfingers evenly with the ½ cup of confectioners' sugar and bake in the middle and upper third of the oven for about 5 minutes, or until the ladyfingers are a delicate gold color and slightly crusty on top.

With a spatula, gently transfer the ladyfingers to cake racks to cool. In Spain, ladyfingers are served with *natillas,* and provide the base for *torta moca* ( *both Recipe Index* ).

# Desserts and Drinks

## Papos de Anjo
### EGG CAKES IN SYRUP

To serve 8

| | |
|---|---|
| 2 tablespoons butter, softened | 2 cups sugar |
| 2 egg whites | 1 cup water |
| 8 egg yolks | 1 teaspoon vanilla extract |

Preheat the oven to 350°. With a pastry brush, coat the bottom and sides of 24 muffin-tin cups with the softened butter. Each cup should be about 2 inches in diameter at the top.

Beat the egg whites with a whisk or a rotary or electric beater until they are firm enough to form unwavering peaks on the beater when it is lifted from the bowl. In a separate bowl and with the same beater, beat the yolks until they thicken enough to fall back on themselves in a slowly dissolving ribbon when the beater is lifted from the bowl. Add the whites to the yolks, and continue beating for about 10 minutes, or until the mixture is very smooth and thick. Then divide it equally among the muffin tins, and set the tins in a large, shallow baking pan. Place the pan on the middle shelf of the oven, and pour enough boiling water into it to come about halfway up the sides of the tins. Bake for about 20 minutes, or until a knife inserted in the center of a cake comes out clean. Let the cakes cool in the tins for 2 to 3 minutes, then gently turn them out onto a large plate and prick each one all the way through in 2 or 3 places with a toothpick. Cool until lukewarm.

In a 1- to 1½-quart saucepan bring the sugar and water to a boil over high heat, stirring until the sugar dissolves. Boil briskly for a minute, then remove the pan from the heat, stir in the vanilla, and pour the syrup into an 11-by-7-inch shallow baking dish. Drop the cakes into the warm syrup, turning them gently about with a spoon to coat them evenly. Cover tightly, refrigerate and let the cakes soak for at least three hours before serving.

Serve the cakes from the baking dish or arrange them on a deep serving plate, and pour the syrup around them.

# Flan de Naranja

ORANGE CARAMEL CUSTARD

To serve 8

CARAMEL

| | |
|---|---|
| 1 cup sugar | ¼ cup water |

To line the bottom of individual custard cups with caramel, it is necessary to work quickly. Because the temperature of hot caramel will be over 300°, handle it with extreme caution. In a small, heavy saucepan or skillet, bring the sugar and water to a boil over high heat, stirring until the sugar completely dissolves. Reduce the heat to moderate and cook briskly without stirring, but gently tipping the pan back and forth until the syrup turns a deep golden brown. This may take 10 minutes or more.

The moment the syrup reaches the desired color, remove the pan from the heat and quickly pour about a tablespoon into the first cup. Tip and swirl the syrup evenly around the bottom, then set the cup aside. In a similar fashion quickly coat the remaining cups with caramel.

CUSTARD

| | |
|---|---|
| 3 small navel oranges | 1 teaspoon vanilla extract |
| 1 quart milk | 6 eggs |
| 2 four-inch pieces of stick cinnamon | 2 egg yolks |
| | 1½ cups sugar |

Preheat the oven to 325°. With a small, sharp knife or rotary peeler, remove the peel from all three oranges without cutting into the bitter white pith underneath it. Set the peel aside. Remove and discard the pith and outside membranes of the oranges. Then free the individual segments of orange, one at a time, by cutting along both sides of the segment down to the center core. Carefully lift out each piece as it is loosened. Set aside.

In a 2- to 3-quart saucepan, bring the milk, orange peel and cinnamon sticks almost to a boil over moderate heat. Remove the pan from the heat, discard the orange peel and cinnamon sticks, and stir in the vanilla.

With a wire whisk, rotary or electric beater, beat the eggs and egg yolks together until well-blended, then add the sugar gradually, and continue to beat until the mixture is thick and pale yellow. Stirring constantly, pour in the hot milk in a thin stream. Then strain it through a fine sieve into a bowl.

Place two or three orange segments in the bottom of each caramel-lined cup and pour in enough custard to come almost to the top. Place the cups in a large, shallow baking pan, and set the pan on the middle shelf of the oven. Pour in enough boiling water to come halfway up the sides of the cups. Bake—lowering the oven temperature if the water in the pan begins to simmer—for about 30 minutes, or until a knife inserted in the center of the custard comes out clean.

Remove the cups from the water and refrigerate for at least 3 hours, or until the custard is thoroughly chilled.

Unmold the custards one at a time. Run a sharp knife around the sides and dip the bottom of the cup briefly in hot water. Wipe the outside of the cup dry, place a chilled serving plate upside down over it and, grasping cup and plate together firmly, quickly turn them over. Rap the plate on a table and the custard should slide easily out of the cup. Pour any extra caramel remaining in the cup over the custard.


## Porto Pudim Flan
PORTUGUESE BAKED CARAMEL CUSTARD

To serve 12

|  |  |
|---|---|
|  | ¾ cup sugar |
| 1½ cups heavy cream | 6 egg yolks |
| 1½ cups milk | 2 teaspoons port |

Preheat the oven to 350°. In a heavy 1- to 1½-quart saucepan warm the cream and milk over high heat until small bubbles appear around the edge of the pan. Set aside off the heat. In a small heavy saucepan or skillet, caramelize the sugar by stirring it over moderate heat, until it melts and turns a light golden brown. Immediately pour the hot cream and milk in a thin stream into the caramel, stirring constantly with a large spoon. Continue to stir until the caramel has thoroughly dissolved.

With a whisk, or a rotary or electric beater, beat the egg yolks until they are well blended. Then slowly pour in the cream mixture, stirring constantly with a spoon. Stir in the port and strain the mixture through a fine sieve into 12 4-ounce heatproof porcelain or glass individual molds or custard cups. Set the molds in a large roasting pan on the middle shelf of the oven and pour in enough boiling water to come halfway up the sides of the molds. Bake for 40 minutes or until a knife inserted in the center of the custard comes out clean. Cool to room temperature, then refrigerate for at least 3 hours, or until thoroughly chilled.

To unmold the custard, run a sharp knife around the inside edge of each mold and dip the bottom briefly in hot water. Then wipe the mold dry, place a chilled serving plate upside down over each mold and, grasping mold and plate firmly together, quickly invert them. Rap the plate on a table and the custard should slide out easily. In Portugal, the custard is sometimes garnished with a flower blossom.

## Natillas

SOFT CUSTARD

To serve 6

| | |
|---|---|
| 3 cups milk | 2 egg yolks |
| 2 cinnamon sticks each 4 inches | ½ cup sugar |
| long | 6 ladyfingers (*page 86*) |
| 4 eggs | Ground cinnamon |

In a heavy 1- to 1½-quart saucepan, heat the milk with the cinnamon sticks until small bubbles begin to form around the edge of the pan. Remove from the heat.

With a whisk or a rotary or electric beater, beat the eggs, egg yolks and sugar in a mixing bowl for 3 or 4 minutes, or until pale yellow and slightly thickened. Beating constantly, slowly pour in the hot milk in a thin stream. Return the mixture to the saucepan. Stirring constantly, cook over low heat until the custard thickens enough to lightly coat the spoon. Do not let the custard come anywhere near a boil or it will curdle. Cool the custard to room temperature.

Just before serving, spoon the custard into six individual dessert dishes, place a ladyfinger in each dish, and sprinkle the custard lightly with ground cinnamon.

## Pastéis de Nata

CUSTARD TARTS

To make 12 three-inch tarts

PASTRY

| | |
|---|---|
| 1 cup all-purpose flour | 1 teaspoon fresh lemon juice |
| ⅛ teaspoon salt | 6 tablespoons unsalted butter, |
| 6 to 8 tablespoons ice water | softened |

Sift the flour and salt together into a large mixing bowl. Sprinkle them with 6 tablespoons of the ice water and the lemon juice and toss together lightly with a fork. Knead the dough with your hands until it is firm enough to be gathered into a compact ball. If the dough crumbles, add up to 2 tablespoons more ice water, 1 teaspoon at a time, until the particles adhere.

On a lightly floured surface, roll the dough into a rectangle about 10 inches long and 8 inches wide. With a metal spatula or your fingers, spread 2 tablespoons of the butter evenly over the pastry. Fold the pastry in thirds in the following fashion: First fold one 8-inch side about 1½ inches beyond the center, then fold the opposite side over the top, reducing the 10-inch dimension to about 3 inches. Turn the pastry around so that an open end faces you and once more roll it out to a 10-inch length and an 8-inch width. Spread the pastry with another 2 tablespoons of butter, and fold it into thirds again. Turn the pastry so that an open end faces you, roll it out to a 10-inch length as before and spread with the remaining 2 tablespoons of butter. Fold in thirds and wrap the pastry in wax paper. Refrigerate for at least 30 minutes before using. (Tightly wrapped, the pastry may be kept in the refrigerator for 3 or 4 days without harm.)

CUSTARD
5 egg yolks
½ cup sugar
1 cup heavy cream

A pinch of salt
2 teaspoons confectioners' sugar
    combined with ¼ teaspoon
    ground cinnamon

Preheat the oven to 400°. In the top of a double boiler, beat the egg yolks with a whisk or a rotary or electric beater until they are well combined. Set the pan over water that is barely simmering and gradually stir in the sugar, cream and salt. Stirring constantly with a wooden spoon, cook over low heat until the mixture thickens enough to coat the spoon lightly. Strain the custard through a fine sieve into a mixing bowl, and cool to room temperature, stirring it now and then to prevent a crust from forming on its surface.

On a lightly floured surface, roll the pastry into an 8- by 10-inch rectangle. With a cookie cutter or the rim of a glass, cut the pastry into 3½-inch rounds. Gather the pastry scraps into a ball, reroll and cut into similar rounds. One at a time, gently press the rounds into individual tart tins measuring 2½ inches in diameter across the bottom.

Spoon the custard into the pastry shells, filling them to within ⅛ inch of the top, then place the tins on a baking sheet. Bake in the middle of the oven for 20 minutes, or until the tops are a light gold color and a knife inserted in the center of the custard comes out clean. Let the tarts cool in the tins for 4 to 5 minutes. Then run the blade of a knife around the edges of the tarts to loosen them slightly, lift them out with a narrow spatula, and sprinkle the tops with the confectioners' sugar and cinnamon mixture. Serve when cooled to room temperature.

## Leche Frita
FRIED CUSTARD SQUARES

To serve 6 to 8

½ cup cornstarch
3 cups milk
½ cup plus 2 tablespoons sugar
2 eggs, lightly beaten
1 cup fine fresh crumbs made
   from French or Italian bread,

trimmed of crusts and
pulverized in a blender or torn
   apart with a fork
4 tablespoons butter
2 tablespoons olive or vegetable oil
1 teaspoon ground cinnamon

In a 1½- to 2-quart saucepan, combine the cornstarch and 1 cup of the milk and stir until the cornstarch dissolves completely. Stir in the remaining 2 cups of milk and ½ cup of the sugar. Bring to a boil over high heat, stirring constantly, and cook briskly until the custard mixture comes to a boil and thickens heavily. Pour the custard into a shallow 8- to 9-inch square baking dish, spread it out evenly with a spatula and refrigerate for at least 4 hours, or until it is firm.

With a knife dipped in hot water, cut the custard into 1¼- to 1½-inch squares. Dip the squares into the beaten eggs and then into the crumbs and place them on a sheet of wax paper. In a heavy 10- to 12-inch skillet, melt the butter in the oil over moderate heat. When the foam begins to subside, add 6 or 8 custard squares and brown them for about 2 minutes on each side, turning them over carefully with a large metal spatula. Transfer them to a heated serving platter and sprinkle with a mixture of the remaining 2 tablespoons of sugar and the cinnamon. Serve hot.

## Queijadas de Évora
SWEET CHEESE TARTS

To make 12 individual 2½-inch tarts

PASTRY
1¼ cups all-purpose flour
2 tablespoons sugar
⅛ teaspoon salt
2 tablespoons chilled butter, cut into

¼-inch pieces
4 tablespoons chilled lard, cut into
   ¼-inch pieces
1 egg, lightly beaten

Preheat the oven to 400°. Sift the flour, 2 tablespoons sugar and ⅛ teaspoon salt into a large, chilled mixing bowl, and add the chilled butter and lard. With your fingertips rub the flour and fat together until they look like flakes of coarse meal. Add the lightly beaten egg and toss together until the dough can be gathered into a compact ball. Wrap in wax paper and chill the dough for at least an hour before using.

On a lightly floured surface, roll the dough into a circle about ⅛ inch thick. With a cookie cutter or the rim of a glass, cut the dough into 3½-inch rounds. Gather the scraps into a ball, reroll and cut into similar rounds. Fit them into ungreased individual tart tins about 2½ inches in diameter and ½ inch deep, and press them gently against the bottom and sides of the tins to form deep shells. Place the tins on a baking sheet and bake in the middle of the oven for 10 minutes, or until the pastry is a delicate gold. Let the shells cool in their tins while you make the filling.

FILLING

| | |
|---|---|
| 3 ounces cream cheese (about ⅓ cup), softened | ¾ cup sugar |
| | 2 egg yolks |
| 1 cup (8 ounces) pot (farmer) cheese | 1½ teaspoons ground cinnamon |
| | ½ teaspoon salt |

FILLING: Reduce the oven heat to 350°. With an electric mixer, beat the cream cheese, pot cheese and sugar together until light and fluffy. Then beat in the egg yolks, cinnamon and ½ teaspoon salt. (To make the filling by hand, cream the cream cheese, pot cheese and sugar together by mashing and beating them against the sides of the bowl with a large spoon until fluffy. Then add the egg yolks, cinnamon and ½ teaspoon salt and continue to beat until smooth.)

Spoon the cheese mixture into the tart shells, dividing it evenly among them and filling the shells to within ¼ inch of their tops. Bake in the middle of the oven for 20 minutes, or until the filling is set and a cake tester inserted in the center comes out clean. Cool the tarts to room temperature, then carefully slip them out of the tins and serve.

NOTE: If you do not have tart tins, bake the tarts in a muffin tin whose cups measure 2½ inches in diameter across the bottom. The pastry rounds will not come completely to the top of the cups, but this will in no way affect the final result.

## Crema Pastelera al Ron

RUM CREAM FILLING

To make about 2 cups

| | |
|---|---|
| 2 cups milk | 2 egg yolks |
| 2 two-inch pieces stick cinnamon | ¼ cup sugar |
| 1 four-inch piece vanilla bean, | ¼ cup flour |
|    broken into ½-inch lengths | 1 tablespoon dark rum |

In a heavy 1- to 1½-quart saucepan, bring the milk, cinnamon stick and vanilla bean to a boil over moderate heat. Cover and set aside off the heat.

In a large mixing bowl, beat the egg yolks and sugar with a whisk or a rotary or electric beater until thick and lemon colored. Beat in the flour 1 tablespoon at a time. Discard the cinnamon stick and vanilla bean and slowly
pour the milk into the egg yolk mixture, beating constantly. Return the mixture to the pan and cook over low heat, stirring constantly with a whisk,
until the mixture comes to a boil and thickens heavily. Stir in the rum and
set aside off the heat to cool to room temperature. Stir every now and then
to prevent a crust from forming on the surface. The cream can be kept in
the refrigerator for 2 or 3 days, before being used as a cake or tart filling.

## Brazo de Gitano

SPONGE CAKE ROLL WITH RUM CREAM FILLING

To make one 15-inch roll

| | |
|---|---|
| 2 tablespoons butter, softened | ⅛ teaspoon salt |
| 6 tablespoons flour | 4 egg whites |
| 4 egg yolks | Rum cream filling *(above)* |
| ¼ cup sugar | Confectioners' sugar |

Preheat the oven to 400°. With a pastry brush, coat the bottom and sides of
a 10½-by-15½-inch jelly-roll pan with 1 tablespoon of butter. Line the pan
with a 20-inch-long strip of wax paper and let the extra paper extend over
the ends. Brush the remaining butter over the paper and sprinkle it with 2 tablespoons of flour, tipping the pan from side to side to spread it evenly.
Turn the pan over and rap it sharply to remove the excess. Set aside.

With a whisk or a rotary or electric beater, beat the egg whites until they
are stiff enough to form unwavering peaks on the beater when it is lifted
from the bowl. In another bowl and with the same beater, beat the egg
yolks, sugar and salt together until thick and lemon colored. Then sprinkle
the remaining 4 tablespoons of flour on top of the egg whites, pour the
yolks over them and, with a rubber spatula, fold together lightly but thor-

oughly, using an over-under cutting motion rather than a stirring motion.

Pour the batter into the pan, spread it into the corners with a spatula, and smooth the top. Bake in the middle of the oven for 8 minutes, or until the cake begins to come away from the sides of the pan. Remove the cake from the oven and carefully turn it out on a fresh sheet of wax paper. Gently peel off the layer of paper on top of the cake and, starting at one long edge, roll the cake into a loose cylinder. Set aside to cool to room temperature.

To assemble the cake, unroll it and spread the top evenly with rum cream filling. Roll up the cake and place it on a serving plate. Just before serving, sprinkle the top and sides of the cake liberally with confectioners' sugar.

## Fatias da China
EGG AND ALMOND SLICES IN SYRUP

To serve 6 to 8

|  |  |
|---|---|
|  | or mortar and pestle |
| 2 teaspoons butter, softened | 1 lemon |
| 8 egg yolks | 2 cups sugar |
| ¼ cup blanched almonds, pulverized | 2 cups water |
| in a blender or with a nut grinder | 2 three-inch pieces of stick cinnamon |

With a pastry brush, coat the bottom and sides of a plain 3-cup heatproof mold (preferably a loaf mold) with the softened butter.

In a large mixing bowl, beat the egg yolks and almonds together with a whisk or a rotary or electric beater until the yolks are thick and lemon colored. Pour the mixture into the mold and cover it tightly with a sheet of buttered foil. Place the mold on a rack in a deep pot, and add boiling water to a depth of 1 inch in the bottom of the pan. Bring to a boil over high heat, cover the pan, reduce the heat to low and simmer for 20 minutes, or until a knife inserted in the center of the egg mixture comes out clean.

Run the blade of a knife around the inside edges of the mold and place an inverted plate over it. Grasping the mold and plate together firmly, turn them over. Rap the plate on a table and the egg loaf should slide out easily. Cut the loaf crosswise into ¼-inch-thick slices. Place the slices in a row, overlapping them slightly, in a deep heatproof serving dish.

With a sharp knife or rotating vegetable peeler, remove the peel of the lemon (without cutting through to the bitter white pith underneath). Cut the peel into strips about 2 inches long and ½ inch wide. Combine the peel, sugar, water and cinnamon sticks in a 1- to 1½-quart saucepan. Bring to a boil over high heat, stirring until the sugar dissolves, then boil briskly, undisturbed, for 5 minutes. Pour the entire contents of the pan over the egg slices. Cool to room temperature, then refrigerate for at least 3 hours, or until thoroughly chilled.

## Pastel de Manzana
APPLE-MINT CRISP

To serve 6

| | |
|---|---|
| 1 tablespoon butter, softened | 1 tablespoon ground cinnamon |
| 1 cup sugar | 4 medium-sized tart cooking apples |
| 1 cup all-purpose flour | (about 2 pounds), peeled, |
| ½ teaspoon double-acting baking | quartered, cored and cut |
| powder | lengthwise into ¼-inch slices |
| 1 egg | 1 cup heavy cream, whipped |
| 1 tablespoon dried mint leaves | (optional) |

Preheat the oven to 350°. With a pastry brush, coat the bottom and sides of an 8-by-8-by-2-inch baking dish with softened butter. Set aside. Combine the sugar, flour and baking powder and sift them into a mixing bowl. Make a well in the center and drop in the egg. Mix together with two table knives until the flour has thoroughly absorbed the egg.

In a large mixing bowl, stir the mint leaves and cinnamon together. Add the apples and toss them about with a large spoon until the slices are evenly coated on all sides. Arrange the slices in the baking dish and scatter the flour mixture over them, spreading and pressing it gently into a smooth layer to cover the apples completely. Bake in the middle of the oven for 45 minutes, or until the topping is crusty. Remove the dish from the oven, cover it tightly with a lid or foil, and set aside to cool. Serve, at room temperature, accompanied if you like with a bowl of whipped cream.

## Torta Moca
MOCHA LAYER CAKE WITH RUM

To make one 7-inch-square cake

| | |
|---|---|
| 8 egg yolks, at room temperature | toasted *( see bôlo de amêndoa à* |
| 1 pound unsalted butter, softened | *algarvia, page 98 )*, 6 of them |
| 1¼ cups sugar | reserved whole for the garnish |
| 2 tablespoons instant *espresso* coffee | and the rest chopped coarsely |
| ½ cup water | 21 four-inch ladyfingers, made |
| 6 tablespoons dark rum | according to the recipe on page |
| ½ cup blanched almonds, lightly | 86, or 21 ready-made ladyfingers |

To make the mocha butter cream, beat the 8 egg yolks in a large bowl with a whisk or a rotary or electric beater until they are thick and lemon colored. Then cream the pound of soft butter by mashing and beating it against the sides of a bowl with a large spoon until it is light and fluffy.

In a small saucepan bring the sugar, coffee and water to a boil, stirring until the sugar and coffee dissolve. Boil briskly without stirring until the syrup thickens and reaches a temperature of 236° on a candy thermometer, or until a drop spooned into cold water immediately forms a soft ball.

Quickly pour the hot syrup in a thin stream into the egg yolks, beating constantly. Continue beating for 10 to 15 minutes longer until the mixture becomes a thick, smooth cream and cools to room temperature. Then beat in the creamed butter, a tablespoon or so at a time. Cover the bowl and refrigerate the cream for at least 30 minutes, or until it becomes firm enough to spread easily.

To assemble the cake, place the ladyfingers flat on a table and cut them in half horizontally. Spread the cut sides of the halves with a thin layer of the butter cream and arrange them cream side down in an approximately square pattern on a large flat serving plate, following the diagram below. Cut two small pieces from another ladyfinger half to fill the empty corner at each side of the square. Spread these pieces lightly with butter cream and set them in place. Sprinkle the top with 1 tablespoon of the rum and spread with about ¼ cup of the butter cream.

Dip the cut sides of 2 more small pieces and 6 more of the ladyfinger halves in the remaining rum and set them in place on top of the square, moistened side down. Spread this layer with butter cream. Repeat to make 6 layers in all, dipping the ladyfingers in rum and spreading them with mocha butter as you proceed.

Mask the top and sides of the cake with the remaining butter cream. If you like, reserve some butter cream to pipe rosettes or swirls around the edge of the cake through a pastry bag fitted with a decorative tip. Gently but firmly press the chopped almonds into the sides of the cake and arrange the whole almonds attractively on top. Refrigerate for at least 4 hours, or until the butter cream is firm.

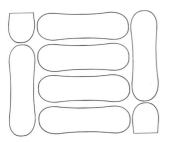

For each layer of the *Torta moca* (*recipe above*), arrange 6 of the ladyfinger halves and 2 small pieces of ladyfinger flat on a serving plate to make an approximately square pattern as shown at left.

## Ovos Moles
EGG YOLK ICING

To make about 1½ cups

1¼ cups sugar

⅓ cup cold water
10 egg yolks

Combine the sugar and water in a 1- to 1½-quart saucepan. Stirring constantly, cook over moderate heat until the sugar is completely dissolved. When the syrup begins to simmer and becomes translucent, remove the pan from the heat and cool to room temperature.

Meanwhile, in a heavy 2- to 3-quart saucepan, beat the egg yolks with a whisk or a rotary or electric beater until they are thick and light yellow. Beating constantly, pour in the syrup in a thin stream. Place the pan over the lowest possible heat and cook, stirring constantly with a large wooden spoon, for about 10 minutes, or until the mixture is smooth and thick enough to coat the spoon heavily. Do not let it come even close to boiling or it may curdle. Strain through a fine sieve set over a bowl and cool to room temperature. The icing will thicken further as it cools.

NOTE: In Portugal, *ovos moles* is not only used as an icing for cakes, but is served as a dessert in individual dessert dishes.

## Bôlo de Amêndoa à Algarvia
ALMOND LAYER CAKE

To make an 11-by-4-inch layer cake

2 tablespoons softened butter
2 tablespoons flour
6 egg whites
A pinch of salt

6 egg yolks
¾ cup sugar
1¾ cups whole blanched almonds
1 teaspoon almond extract
*Ovos moles (above)*

Preheat the oven to 350°. Using a pastry brush coat the bottom and sides of an 11-by-17-inch jelly-roll pan with 1 tablespoon of softened butter. Line the pan with a 22-inch-long strip of wax paper allowing the extra paper to extend 2 inches over each end. Brush the remaining butter evenly over the paper, then sprinkle with 2 tablespoons of flour and tip the pan from side to side to spread the flour evenly. Now turn the pan over and rap it sharply on a table to remove the excess.

Place the almonds on a baking sheet and toast them in the middle of the oven for about 10 minutes, or until they color lightly. Set ¼ cup aside and pulverize the rest in a blender or with a nut grinder or mortar and pestle.

In a large mixing bowl, beat the egg whites and salt with a whisk or a rotary or electric beater until they form firm unwavering peaks on the beater when it is lifted from the bowl. In a separate bowl, beat the egg yolks and sugar with the same beater until the mixture thickens enough to fall back on itself in a slowly dissolving ribbon when the beater is lifted from the bowl. Then stir the pulverized almonds and the teaspoon of almond extract into the beaten egg yolks.

Mix about one fourth of the egg whites into the yolks and pour them over the remaining egg whites. With a rubber spatula, fold together, gently but thoroughly, using an over-and-under cutting motion rather than a stirring motion. Pour the batter into the pan, spread it into the corners with the spatula, and smooth the top.

Bake in the middle of the oven for 15 to 20 minutes, or until the cake is light gold and has begun to come away from the sides of the pan. Remove the cake from the oven and let it cool in the pan for 2 or 3 minutes. Then carefully turn it out on a fresh sheet of wax paper. Gently peel off the top layer of paper and let the cake cool to room temperature before frosting it.

To assemble the cake, trim the crusts from the edges with a large, sharp knife and slice the cake crosswise into four 11-by-4-inch rectangles. Place a rectangular layer of cake on a serving plate and, with a metal spatula or knife, spread it evenly with ¼ cup of the *ovos moles* icing. Set a second layer on top, spread with another ¼ cup of the icing and repeat the layers of cake and icing. Place the last layer of cake on top and spread the top and sides with the remaining *ovos moles*. Arrange the ¼ cup of whole almonds decoratively in two parallel rows along the length of the cake. Serve at once or let the cake rest at room temperature for 2 or 3 hours to absorb the icing.

## Toucinho do Céu

"BACON FROM HEAVEN" ALMOND CAKE

To make an 8-inch round cake

| | |
|---|---|
| 2 tablespoons butter, softened | 8 egg yolks |
| 4 tablespoons plus 2 cups sugar | 1½ teaspoons almond extract |
| 2½ cups whole blanched almonds | 1 teaspoon ground cinnamon |
| 9 tablespoons water | 1 teaspoon finely grated lemon peel |

Preheat the oven to 350°. With a pastry brush, coat the bottom and sides of an 8-inch springform cake pan with the butter. Then add 2 tablespoons of the sugar, tipping the pan from side to side to spread it evenly on the bottom and sides. Turn the pan over and rap it sharply to remove the excess.

Spread the almonds on a baking sheet and toast them in the middle of the oven for about 10 minutes or until they color lightly. Remove the nuts from the oven and increase the heat to 375°. Set ¼ cup of the nuts aside and pulverize the rest in a blender or with a nutgrinder or mortar and pestle.

In a heavy 1- to 1½-quart saucepan, bring 2 cups of the sugar and the water to a boil over moderate heat, stirring until the sugar dissolves. Add the pulverized almonds and, stirring constantly, cook for about 5 minutes or until the mixture comes to a boil and becomes translucent. So that it will cool more quickly, pour the syrup into a bowl or another pan and set it aside until it is lukewarm.

In a heavy 3- to 4-quart saucepan, beat the egg yolks with a whisk or a rotary or electric beater until they are thick and lemon colored. Still beating, pour in the lukewarm almond mixture in a thin stream and continue to beat until cool and thick. Add the almond extract, cinnamon and lemon peel and place the pan over the lowest possible heat. Cook, stirring constantly, for about 15 minutes, or until the mixture is thick enough to coat the spoon heavily. Do not allow it to boil or the eggs will curdle.

Pour the mixture into the pan and sprinkle the top evenly with the remaining 2 tablespoons of sugar. Bake in the middle of the oven for 15 to 20 minutes or until the cake is firm to the touch. Then remove it from the oven and let cool for 10 minutes before removing the cake from the pan. Serve warm, or at room temperature, sprinkled immediately before serving with a little more sugar and topped with the reserved toasted almonds.

## *Arroz Doce*
RICE PUDDING

To serve 4 to 6

| | |
|---|---|
| | 6 cups water |
| 1½ cups milk | ½ cup raw medium or long-grain |
| A 2-inch piece of vanilla bean | regular-milled rice or imported |
| A 2-inch piece of stick cinnamon | short-grain rice |
| 6 pieces lemon peel, each about | 3 egg yolks |
| 1½ inches long and ½ inch wide | ⅓ cup sugar |
| ⅛ teaspoon plus ¼ teaspoon salt | 1 teaspoon ground cinnamon |

In a 1- to 1¼-quart saucepan, bring the milk, vanilla bean, cinnamon stick, pieces of lemon peel and ⅛ teaspoon of the salt to a boil over moderate heat. Cover the pan tightly, remove it from the heat and let the seasonings steep for 20 to 30 minutes.

Meanwhile, bring 6 cups of water to a boil in a 2- to 3-quart saucepan. Pour in the rice in a slow stream, stirring constantly, so that the water continues to boil. Add the remaining ¼ teaspoon of salt, reduce the heat to moderate, and boil the rice uncovered 15 to 20 minutes, or until tender. Drain the rice in a colander, turning it about with a fork to separate the grains, then spread it out on a double thickness of paper towels.

In a large bowl, beat the egg yolks and sugar together with a whisk or a rotary or electric beater until light and lemon colored. Beating constantly, pour in the milk in a thin stream. Then return the mixture to the saucepan and cook over low heat, stirring constantly with a wooden spoon until the custard thickens enough to coat the spoon lightly. Do not let it come anywhere near the boil or it may curdle. Remove the vanilla bean and cinnamon stick, add the rice to the custard and cook over low heat for 2 minutes, stirring constantly with a fork. Pour the pudding into a deep platter or a baking dish about 12-by-8 inches and no more than ½ inch deep. Cool to room temperature and just before serving, sprinkle the top lightly with cinnamon.

NOTE: In Portugal it is traditional to sprinkle the cinnamon through a hand-cut paper doily to form a pattern on the rice. If you like, use a ready-made doily.

# Buñuelos de Plátano

DEEP-FRIED BANANA FRITTERS

To serve 4 to 6

1 cup flour
¼ teaspoon salt
1 egg, lightly beaten
1 tablespoon butter, melted
½ cup milk
1 egg white
2 tablespoons sugar

¼ cup dark rum or brandy
6 firm ripe bananas, peeled and cut
    lengthwise in half, then crosswise
    into quarters
Vegetable oil or shortening for deep-
    fat frying
Confectioners' sugar

To prepare the batter, sift ½ cup of the flour and the salt into a deep mixing bowl. Stir in the beaten egg and butter and then the milk and continue to stir until the batter is smooth. Do not beat or overstir. For the best results, set the batter aside at room temperature and let it rest for an hour or so, although it may be used at once if it must. In either case, the egg white should be beaten with a whisk or rotary beater until stiff and then folded into the batter just before using it.

Meanwhile, in a large bowl, combine the sugar and rum or brandy, and stir until the sugar dissolves. Drop in the bananas and turn them about with a spoon until they are thoroughly moistened. Set aside at room temperature for 30 minutes, turning the bananas occasionally.

Heat 3 to 4 inches of oil or shortening in a deep-fat fryer or large heavy skillet until it reaches 375° on a deep-frying thermometer. Pat the pieces of banana dry with paper towels, dip them in the remaining ½ cup of flour and shake vigorously to remove the excess. With tongs, dip them into the batter and then deep-fry them, 5 or 6 at a time, for 2 or 3 minutes, or until golden brown on all sides. Transfer the fried fritters to paper towels and let them drain while you fry the remaining bananas. Serve warm, liberally sprinkled with confectioners' sugar.


# Bomboms de Figos

FIG CANDIES WITH ALMONDS

To make about 30

½ cup whole blanched almonds

1 pound dried figs

Preheat the oven to 350°. Spread the almonds evenly in a baking dish and toast them in the middle of the oven, for about 10 minutes, or until they are lightly browned. Turn them occasionally so that they brown well on all sides. With a large, sharp knife, coarsely chop half of the almonds. Then set the whole and chopped nuts aside separately to cool.

With a small knife, cut off and discard the stems of the figs. Chop the figs coarsely, and purée them through a food mill set over a bowl. To make each *bombom*, butter the palms of your hands lightly and roll about 1 teaspoon of the puréed figs into a ball. Insert a whole almond into the ball, and continue to shape and pat it until the nut is completely enclosed. Roll the *bombom* in the chopped almonds to coat it thoroughly and set aside on wax paper. Proceed similarly with the remaining figs and almonds. Fig *bomboms* are traditionally served after dinner, accompanied by glasses of port.


## Figos Recheados

DRIED FIGS STUFFED WITH ALMONDS AND CHOCOLATE

To make 12

| | |
|---|---|
| | 12 large dried figs |
| ¼ cup plus 12 whole blanched almonds | ½ ounce (½ square) semisweet chocolate, finely grated |

Preheat the oven to 350°. Place the almonds on a baking sheet and toast them in the middle of the oven for about 10 minutes, or until they color lightly. Set 12 of the almonds aside and pulverize the rest in a blender or in a nut grinder or with mortar and pestle.

With scissors or a small knife, cut the stems off the figs. Then with your finger or the handle of a small spoon, make a ½-inch depression in the stem end of each fig. Mix the pulverized almonds and chocolate and stuff about 1 teaspoon of the mixture into each fig. Pinch the openings together firmly. Arrange the figs stem side up on an ungreased baking sheet and bake in the middle of the oven for 5 minutes. Turn the figs over with tongs and bake for another 5 minutes.

Press a toasted almond gently but firmly into the opening of each fig and serve at once or cool to room temperature before serving. *Figos recheados* are traditionally served after dinner, accompanied by glasses of port.

## Limonada

BASQUE RED AND WHITE WINE "LEMONADE"

To serve 8

6 lemons
1 cup superfine sugar
1 bottle dry red wine, preferably
imported Spanish wine
1 bottle dry white wine, preferably
imported Spanish wine

With a small, sharp knife or a vegetable peeler with rotating blade, remove the yellow peel from three of the lemons, being careful not to cut into the bitter white pith underneath it. Cut the peel into strips about 2 inches long and ½ inch wide. Set them aside. Squeeze the juice from one of the peeled lemons and then slice the remaining 3 unpeeled lemons crosswise into ¼-inch-thick rounds.

Combine the strips of lemon peel, the lemon juice, lemon slices and sugar in a 3- to 4-quart serving pitcher. Pour in the red and white wine and stir with a bar spoon or other long-handled spoon until well mixed. Refrigerate for at least 8 hours, stirring two or three times.

To serve, stir again, taste and add more sugar if you prefer the drink sweeter. Serve in chilled wine glasses or tumblers. If you like, the glasses may be filled with ice cubes before adding the *limonada*.

## Sangría

RED WINE AND FRUIT PUNCH

To serve 4 to 6

½ lemon, cut into ¼-inch slices
½ orange, cut into ¼-inch slices
½ large apple, cut in half lengthwise, cored, and cut into thin wedges
¼ to ½ cup superfine sugar
1 bottle dry red wine, preferably
imported Spanish wine
2 ounces (¼ cup) brandy
Club soda, chilled
Ice cubes (optional)

Combine the lemon, orange, apple and ¼ cup sugar in a large pitcher. Pour in the wine and brandy and stir with a long-handled spoon until well mixed. Taste. If you prefer the *sangría* sweeter, add up to ¼ cup more sugar.

Refrigerate for at least 1 hour or until thoroughly chilled. Just before serving, pour in chilled club soda to taste, adding up to 24 ounces of the soda. Stir again, and serve at once in chilled wine glasses. Or the glasses may be filled with ice cubes before adding the *sangría*.

# Recipe Index: English

## Soups

## Seafood

## Meats

# Poultry and Game Birds

# Egg Dishes

# Vegetables, Rice, Salads and Sauces

# Breads, Crullers and Cookies

# Desserts and Drinks

# Recipe Index: Spanish and Portuguese

## Soups

## Seafood

## Meats

## Poultry and Game Birds

## Egg Dishes

## Vegetables, Rice, Salads and Sauces

## Breads, Crullers and Cookies

## Desserts and Drinks

Notes

Drawings and illustrations by Matt Greene.